THE
Cash Flow
Management
Book *for*
Nonprofits

THE
Cash Flow Management Book *for* Nonprofits

A Step-by-Step Guide for Managers, Consultants, and Boards

by
Murray Dropkin, CPA, M.B.A.
and
Allyson Hayden, M.S.W., C.S.W.

JOSSEY-BASS
A Wiley Company
www.josseybass.com

Published by

JOSSEY-BASS
A Wiley Company
989 Market Street
San Francisco, CA 94103-1741

www.josseybass.com

Jossey-Bass books and products are available through most bookstores. To contact Jossey-Bass directly, call (888) 378-2537, fax to (800) 605-2665, or visit our website at www.josseybass.com.

Substantial discounts on bulk quantities of Jossey-Bass books are available to corporations, professional associations, and other organizations. For details and discount information, contact the special sales department at Jossey-Bass.

We at Jossey-Bass strive to use the most environmentally sensitive paper stocks available to us. Our publications are printed on acid-free recycled stock whenever possible and our paper always meets or exceeds minimum GPO and EPA requirements.

Library of Congress Cataloging-in-Publication Data

Dropkin, Murray.
      The cash flow management book for nonprofits: a step-by-step guide for managers, consultants, and boards / by Murray Dropkin and Allyson Hayden.
         p. cm.
      ISBN 0-7879-5385-7 (alk. paper)
      1. Nonprofit organizations—Finance. 2. Cash flow. 3. Nonprofit organizations—Management. I. Hayden, Allyson. II. Title.

HG4027.65 .D763 2001
658.15—dc21

2001040759

PB Printing   10 9 8 7 6 5 4 3 2 1   FIRST EDITION

The Jossey-Bass
Nonprofit & Public Management Series

CONTENTS

LIST OF EXHIBITS

Chapter Seventeen

Chapter Eighteen

Chapter Nineteen

Chapter Twenty

Resource A

Resource B

This book is dedicated to the memory of Bill La Touche, a great friend and colleague. Bill devoted much of his professional and personal life to helping nonprofits and their staffs and clients. He was devoted to helping people at any time of the day, any day, any year. We are not going to say more because Bill himself was a very modest person. He was coauthor of *The Budget-Building Book for Nonprofits* and passed away before he could see a bound copy. We hope this book can continue in the tradition of our professional collaboration, which encompassed more than two decades.

Preface

Successful management of nonprofit organizations has become more and more complicated over the past four decades. Every aspect of the nonprofit environment has undergone, and continues to undergo, many changes. The ways in which government, foundations, and individual donors support nonprofits are constantly evolving. Regulation of nonprofits has been intensifying. The need for services has increased, both in quantity and breadth. Recent media attention has created a greater public demand for accountability. And for many nonprofits these issues are further complicated by reductions in government-sponsored social service programs. All of these circumstances have contributed to the financial and management challenges now faced by many organizations. Increasingly, nonprofits are finding that they must develop new strategies for generating income to remain effective in meeting the needs of our nation's most vulnerable populations. In many instances organizations have risen to the occasion and have been able to maintain (and even expand on) the high level of services they offer, despite the environmental challenges.

We have worked with thousands of nonprofit organizations over the last thirty-five years, providing services and consultation in the areas of auditing, taxation, management and organizational development, and other finance-related operations. We have been continually impressed by our clients' ability to adapt, thrive, grow, and increase their income to meet internal and external demands.

The changes in the operating environment and the added pressures just described have affected the way nonprofit organizations function. Virtually every aspect of nonprofit programmatic, procedural, and financial operations has felt the impact. Those who work with and in nonprofits must respond by adopting new perspectives and approaches that take these considerations into account. Organizations have to learn to function at a higher level of efficiency to remain viable, to serve their purposes, and to obtain the resources they need. We believe that two of the most important financial management tools for achieving these objectives are effective budgeting and effective cash flow planning and management.

Improving budgeting processes and cash flow management helps organizations succeed. Improving these financial operations also helps nonprofits increase income, which is the best way of improving cash flow. However, generating income will not by itself result in improving cash flow. Organizations must become "profitable." Holding an expensive fundraising event to increase income will not substantially benefit your organization's cash flow unless you are "turning a profit." Unfortunately, this is a concept that is often overlooked. In their efforts to quickly remedy cash flow problems, organizations sometimes opt for what seems like the easiest solution instead of the most profitable. For example, when faced with cash shortages, some organizations will engage in extreme cost-cutting measures as their primary intervention. We would be terribly remiss in this discussion if we failed to note that in the long run such measures are likely to backfire. Peter F. Drucker, in his groundbreaking book *Managing for Results* (HarperCollins, 1964), addresses this concept. Drucker explains that costs cannot actually be "cut" for enduring results. In reality, major cost cutting frequently leads to higher costs in eighteen months or less after the cuts are implemented. People devise ways to keep operations going by circumventing the cost cutters. For example, organizations that lay off or fire several clerical staff members will often end up hiring "temps" at the request of executives who need administrative support. Ultimately, the temps prove to be more expensive and less effective in performing their functions than the cut clerical staff was. The key to real cost cutting, Drucker says, is determining which of your organization's operations are not working or are compromising the organization's success and then modifying or completely abandoning such programs or activities. For example, your nonprofit may have been the first organization in town to offer individuals with AIDS special social services. Perhaps a new health agency is now offering similar but more comprehensive services to the same population. Your organization needs to determine with proper research if the services you offer, which were innovative fifteen years ago, are still necessary in your community. You may find that your organization's services are redundant or, worse, not really responsive to your clients' current needs. Once this information is available, your organization will be able to make the very difficult decision whether or not to discontinue the program (or to merge it with another agency's program).

As already stated, research and the history of most organizations indicate that it is nearly impossible to really cut costs. What *is* possible is to set up mechanisms to examine what clients, customers, or communities need on an ongoing basis. The results of these assessments allow your organization to modify or cease the functions that are no longer best performed by your organization and to design appropriate new programs for serving your clients. We also strongly suggest that your organization use the Drucker Foundation Self-Assessment Tool, published by Jossey-Bass, to help accomplish these analyses.

Organizations must learn to operate as effectively and as efficiently as possible. Operating effectively means that organizations are fulfilling their missions and best serving their clients. Operating efficiently means that organizations are devoting the greatest possible amount of their resources to fulfilling their missions. It also means that organizations have what it takes to increase income and remain fiscally sound. Ultimately, greater efficiency will mean that organizations will have a greater amount of financial resources with which to increase their impact on society.

In researching background information for preparing this book, we came across a number of technical and scholarly texts on financial management. However, we were unable to find a book that offered practical advice on financial management and cash flow, specifically geared toward the nonprofit community. It is our sincere hope that *The Cash Flow Management Book for Nonprofits* will fill this gap and, in doing so, help organizations fulfill their goals.

August 2001   Murray Dropkin
Brooklyn, New York   Allyson Hayden

ACKNOWLEDGMENTS

W e would like to express our appreciation to Shawn M. Stack and Eric Havemann for their contributions to this book. We are most grateful for their editorial input and assistance.

We would also like to thank the following people for their time, effort, and encouragement as we researched, wrote, reviewed, and revised *The Cash Flow Management Book for Nonprofits:* David Freed, president and CEO, Nyack Hospital; George Gerharz; Sharon Grant; Jim Halpin; Philip M. Henry, publishing consultant and freelance writer and editor; Edward Kitrosser of Turnquist, Schmitt, Kitrosser & McMahon; Sylvan Leabman; Steven Mildener; Scott Phillips; Marianne Pessognelli; Leona Terry; Ronald J. Werthman, vice president of finance, treasurer, and CFO, Johns Hopkins Health System Corporation; Michael Wojciehowski; Carol Wolff, executive director, Camden Area Health Education Center; and August V. Zolfo.

We also want to express our sincere gratitude to Tom Burgin; Marietta Carstarphen; Eusebio David; Shirley Dey; Theresa Dominianni; Everard Digges La Touche; Michael Leggiero, president and CEO, and Michelle DeSocio, CFO, North Hudson Community Action Corporation; Barbara Lowry, executive director, and Kurt Lindsay, controller, Northern Manhattan Improvement Corporation; James G. McGiffin, executive director, Wendy Kolb, business manager, and Barbara Starling, board member, Community Legal Aid Society, Inc.; Vincent Milito of Sarowitz & Milito; Danny Mims; Mel Nusbaum; Ralph Porter; Dave Reid, Jr.; and Mary Sulliali.

Rachel Anderson, our production editor, supplied professional guidance and suggestions. We appreciated her very important collaborative role. We also are appreciative of Dorothy Hearst and her colleagues at Jossey-Bass Publishers for all their help and support in publishing this book.

We also thank Goldie and Lisa Dropkin Stephan and Chase Hayden.

THE AUTHORS

Murray Dropkin is president of CMS Systems, Inc., a consulting firm that specializes in improving the operational and financial systems of nonprofit organizations. Dropkin is a certified public accountant in New York, New Jersey, and Wisconsin and is managing partner, Dropkin & Company, Certified Public Accountants. He has thirty-five years of experience in accounting, auditing, taxation, and management consulting for government, commercial, and nonprofit organizations ranging in size from $250,000 to $2 billion in annual revenue. Dropkin is coauthor of *The Budget-Building Book for Nonprofits* (Jossey-Bass, 1998), used by the American Institute of Certified Public Accountants in designing group and self-study courses. He is coauthor of *Guide to Audits of Nonprofit Organizations* (three volumes, published annually since 1989 by Practitioners Publishing), coeditor of the monthly newsletter *Nonprofit Report*, and author of articles published in professional accounting journals. Dropkin is a member of the American Institute of Certified Public Accountants, the Association of Government Accountants, and the New York and New Jersey State Certified Public Accountants Societies. He has served on the American Institute of Certified Public Accountant's committee on tax-exempt organizations and on the national board of directors of Accountants for the Public Interest. He has also served as a member of the New York State Charities Registration Advisory Committee. Dropkin holds an M.B.A. from New York University and a B.S. from Brooklyn College. He can be reached at murray@dropkin.com.

Allyson Hayden is a senior consultant, editor, and writer for CMS Systems, Inc. She has fifteen years of experience in writing for commercial and professional magazines, newsletters, and other publications in the areas of organizational development, health, medicine, fundraising, accounting, sociology, and psychology. She has designed workshops, training seminars, and educational materials for nonprofit and accounting organizations, is coeditor of *Nonprofit Report*, and has coauthored a variety of published materials for CMS Systems, Inc. Hayden is a clinical social worker and has served as a group facilitator, team leader, and supervisor in social work program analysis, development, and implementation in the areas of client advocacy, mental health, and civil rights. She holds an M.S.W. from New York University and a B.S. from Brooklyn College.

INTRODUCTION

*T*he *Cash Flow Management Book for Nonprofits* was developed to help organizations improve cash flow management and, ultimately, increase income. Organizations that manage cash flow effectively will also reap the benefit of greater overall management efficiency. The goal of *The Budget-Building Book for Nonprofits* (by Murray Dropkin and Bill La Touche; Jossey-Bass, 1998) was to provide comprehensive instructions and information on sound budget development. The methodologies explained in *The Budget-Building Book for Nonprofits* may be considered a foundation for effective financial management. Proper cash flow planning and management will make operating budgets more than just documents that collect dust on a shelf. Using budgets to guide overall financial management—especially cash flow planning and management—is the way organizations can truly become more effective.

The Cash Flow Management Book for Nonprofits starts where *The Budget-Building Book for Nonprofits* leaves off. Budgets provide a framework for overall financial management and operations. Cash flow forecasts that grow out of effective operating budgets can be used to guide the day-to-day financial functioning of organizations. Optimizing cash flow should always be one of the most important considerations in practical financial decision making.

Effective cash flow planning and management are essential to achieving your organization's mission—its very reason for existence. The best long-term strategic plans will fail if payrolls are missed because of insufficient cash. Unfortunately, many organizations learn about how important effective cash flow management is to their missions the hard way. In our experience as consultants, we have seen organizations that were forced to curtail major activities, merge with another nonprofit, or completely cease operations after long-term cash flow mismanagement.

The cash flow management needs and concerns of nonprofits will vary based on the size and structure of the organization. For example, smaller organizations may have a part-time volunteer CFO who has primary responsibility for cash flow oversight. Larger organizations may have hundreds or even thousands of people who are part of their financial management systems. In developing *The Cash Flow Management Book for Nonprofits,* we have tried to keep in mind the diverse needs of our potential readers. Of course, organizations should modify our suggestions to match their needs and capabilities, especially regarding the implementation of new procedures.

How This Book Is Organized

The Cash Flow Management Book for Nonprofits is divided into five parts to help you find the most relevant information for your organization, no matter what your needs, level of experience, or familiarity with cash flow issues. Part One provides an overview of the importance of cash flow planning and management for nonprofits, reviewing the requirements, controls, and other considerations affecting cash flow planning and management. Part One includes a reference guide to help readers find the chapters in this book that are most relevant to their needs quickly and easily (see Exhibit 2.1). Part One also includes a detailed description of a nonprofit organization that we call "Universal Nonprofit," which will be referred to throughout the book to help illustrate some important cash flow concepts. Universal Nonprofit, introduced in Chapter One, has cash flow concerns that will be relevant to many organizations. We hope that by supplying our readers with concrete examples such as this one, the cash flow strategies that we suggest will be easier to understand and apply in the real world.

Part Two contains information and instructions on improving overall cash flow planning and management and on increasing income. Part Two includes chapters on developing policies and procedures, developing, monitoring, and reporting cash flow forecasts, improving cash flow, and planning for capital projects.

In Part Three you will find detailed information on cash flow forecasting, planning, and management for specific classifications of income. Part Three includes nine chapters, each covering a different type of income for nonprofit organizations. For each of the income classifications, we provide specific and comprehensive techniques for improving cash flow management, related to both cost reduction and income enhancement. Part Three also features useful information on a range of critical issues—cash flow forecasting, planning, reporting, monitoring, and analysis, common cash flow problems and solutions, technology issues, and special considerations—specific to each category of income. Your organization's operations and sources of income will determine which of the chapters in Part Three will be relevant to you.

Part Four offers a summary of the importance of cash flow management and practical advice on how information contained in *The Cash Flow Management Book for Nonprofits* can be integrated into your organization's cash management strategy. Part Four also includes a sample cash flow improvement plan, which illustrates many of the concepts addressed throughout the book.

Part Five includes checklists, sample forms, worksheets, and other tools to get your organization started in developing a cash flow management plan based on the strategies contained in this book.

In referring to various types of cash inflow (or "income") throughout this book, we have chosen to use terminology in a way that might be somewhat different from the way finance professionals would use this terminology. We have done this to make the book more accessible to those without accounting backgrounds. For example, accountants use a number of different terms to distinguish types of cash inflow, such as *support, revenue, gains,* and *income.* We use the terms *income, revenue,* and *cash inflow* to describe moneys received by organizations.

In addition, we have avoided using terms related to treasury functions, even though such terminology is often used in business and in certain nonprofits. For example, larger nonprofits may have an executive in the position of "treasurer" whose responsibility it is to manage cash flow and financing operations. For ease of reference, we have generally used the term *CFO,* but discussions of a CFO's functions pertain equally to any financial manager in small, large, or midsize nonprofits.

Finally, we have tried to find a middle ground regarding technical and organizational issues. As this book is a primer on a specific aspect of financial operations, we have attempted to make it accessible and understandable to the majority of potential readers. Those requiring more technical information will be able to find it in specialized financial texts dealing with cash flow.

THE
Cash Flow
Management
Book *for*
Nonprofits

PART ONE

Cash Flow Management: Overview

THIS SECTION OF THE BOOK provides an overview of the importance of cash flow planning and management for nonprofits. It reviews the requirements, controls, and other considerations that affect cash flow planning and management. Chapter One includes a detailed description of "Universal Nonprofit," a hypothetical organization used as a model throughout the book to illustrate important cash flow concepts. In Chapter Two you will find a quick reference guide for locating the chapters in this book that will be most helpful to your organization.

The Importance of Proper Cash Flow Management

Effective cash flow management is vital to nonprofits; it is a key element in planning and in the efficient functioning of all aspects of operations. The phrase "cash is king" is as applicable in the nonprofit sector as it is in the business sector. Earning income is a primary concern (or should be) for both nonprofit and for-profit entities. However, "making money," although of major importance to ensuring good cash flow, is not the only significant aspect of cash flow management. When cash inflows and outflows—money received and money paid out—are not successfully planned and monitored, organizations may not be able to pay employees and vendors in a timely manner. Thus, without good cash flow management, an organization may be "profitable" based on its financial statements yet unable to pay bills when they are due. For example, an organization may have billed counseling clients a total of $50,000 over three months. Based on the organization's revenue versus cost for providing these services, it may be showing a "profit." However, if clients pay their bills slowly or not at all, this organization may still be unable to meet its payroll.

A. How Can Nonprofits Benefit from Effective Cash Flow Management?

Effective cash flow management can be "profitable" in and of itself. Cash shortages result in increased costs, such as interest charges on loans, late-payment penalties, and loss of vendor discounts for paying bills promptly. Cash flow improvements can eliminate these costs and create the opportunity for more favorable payment terms on some types of purchases. Ultimately, organizations that improve the manner in which they receive and expend cash will be more successful. They will also be able to increase their income.

B. What Issues Are Important in Cash Flow Management?

Unique circumstances in many nonprofits make cash flow management a complicated task. Our more than three decades of work with a wide variety of nonprofits, from "store-front" agencies to billion-dollar institutions, have shown us the necessity of understanding the different cash flow characteristics of nonprofit organizations. For example, in a typical for-profit business with $1 million of annual revenue, there may only be one source for the revenue (such as sales of merchandise or fees for services). Frequently, a nonprofit with the same amount of revenue will have several different sources of income.

The types of income an organization receives determine the cash flow management issues that will be most important. In turn, these particular cash flow issues will determine the strategy that must be used to improve cash flow management. For example, the budgeting, cash flow planning, and cash flow management strategies of nonprofits that depend on contributions as their primary source of income will be quite different from those of organizations that collect fees for services. Nonprofits that are primarily grant funded will have their own unique challenges in managing cash flow. These differences and the ways they can be handled most effectively are the basis for *The Cash Flow Management Book for Nonprofits*.

C. Who Will Benefit from a Better Understanding of Cash Flow Management?

The Cash Flow Management Book for Nonprofits was written to assist all who are involved in the financial management of nonprofit organizations. It is meant to be a comprehensive guide for:

- Identifying and understanding an organization's cash flow characteristics, strengths, and weaknesses
- Creating cash flow forecasts and using other tools for more effective cash flow planning and management
- Improving cash flow through implementing relevant strategies
- Using cash flow information to improve overall operations

D. Who Should Be Involved in Cash Flow Management?

Ideally, all staff, management, and board members of nonprofits should develop a "cash flow awareness." Everyone in your organization can help improve cash flow by understanding the relevant issues. For example, line staff may often be involved in making purchases for the organization. If a staff member fails to follow proper procurement policies and procedures, it will affect cash flow negatively. The same would be true if a staff member found out about a sale of office products and made a bulk purchase, thinking this purchase was saving the organization money in the long run. However, if this cash outflow was not in the cash flow forecast, the organization could have a problem paying the large unexpected bill. In order for line staff to use effective procedures for purchasing, policies must exist, be understood, and be supported. When staff lacks clear guidelines, lacks understanding, or does not support policies, cash flow will be compromised.

Staff and board members must understand their roles in effective cash flow management. Staff and management at every level can become more involved in improving cash flow if cash flow issues are regularly addressed during staff meetings. Creating an ongoing forum for awareness, questions, and feedback can help ensure that everyone is working toward the common goal of cash flow improvement.

All staff members in nonprofit organizations should have an awareness of basic cash flow issues. Personnel who are more directly involved in planning and managing cash flow must allocate time specifically for cash flow planning and management. Such personnel often include finance department staff, fundraising staff, the CEO, the CFO, program staff, and the board of directors. Organizations would see a dramatic improvement in their fiscal health if those who are involved in managing cash flow gave it the same level of priority as they do in their personal lives.

E. An Example

A number of different management theories, concepts, and methods have come and gone since management formally became a topic of study in the nineteenth century, beginning with Frederick W. Taylor's work. One approach Taylor employed that we believe is timeless is the use of "stories" to help provide context in applying management theories to real-world situations. Our story concerns a hypothetical nonprofit organization, "Universal Nonprofit," that is experiencing a number of cash flow–related problems. Universal Nonprofit's characteristics and the interventions we recommend to this hypothetical organization are composites of the characteristics of the many organizations for which we have worked and the recommendations we have made as consultants. The purpose of including this story is to help illustrate the more complex concepts we present throughout the book. You will notice that some of the examples we provide in later chapters use as a point of reference the circumstances we describe here for Universal Nonprofit.

The Universal Nonprofit Story

Universal Nonprofit is a medium-sized nonprofit organization located in a suburban area just outside of a large city. The organization has existed for ten years and has grown considerably in that time from a one-program grassroots health clinic to a multiservice community center offering a variety of comprehensive services to economically disadvantaged community residents. We will assume that Universal Nonprofit engaged our services as consultants to address what it described as a "severe cash flow problem."

Universal Nonprofit depends on a number of sources for income. It receives two large federal grants and a smaller state grant (which support two programs), has a small endowment as the result of a major-donor drive several years ago, enjoys ongoing support from a foundation, and receives several annual corporate grants. In addition, Universal Nonprofit bills for some of its medical and mental health services.

The CEO made it clear that our primary task would be to find some solutions quickly, as the organization was having difficulty paying its bills. After a few interviews with staff at various levels, it became clear that the issue was not just cash flow: a significant overall financial management problem existed and was causing the cash flow problem. Our analysis of the organization's operations uncovered errors in the financial reporting system, a lack of cash flow forecasts sufficiently detailed to properly monitor cash flow, and poor billing and collection methods. Moreover, we found that Universal Nonprofit's inventories were not properly managed and that large amounts of operating funds had been invested in assets that were not readily convertible to cash.

We concluded that cash flow planning and management had never been a priority for Universal Nonprofit. As we began working to develop solutions, our understanding that cash flow is not one financial management issue but is linked to and embedded in the overall financial management of organizations was demonstrated over and over again. We found that many of our solutions to cash flow problems involved a lot more than just fixing cash flow. It became apparent that improving overall financial management, especially in its relationship to cash flow management, would be the only way of ensuring long-term financial stability and solvency.

Real experience garnered from our consulting work with organizations much like Universal Nonprofit is incorporated into many of the examples used in this book. Moreover, in several cases, we present specific strategies and materials we created in the course of our professional work. For example, the grant checklist for cash flow planning and management presented in Resource B was originally developed to help an organization much like Universal Nonprofit improve grant cash flow management, and Chapter Twenty details the steps that organization took to improve its cash flow management.

CHAPTER 2

Types of Nonprofit Income: Financial and Cash Flow Management Considerations

The nature of a nonprofit's income is the single most important factor in determining its overall financial management. All organizations, for-profit and nonprofit alike, need cash to operate. The manner in which organizations obtain cash and the form in which cash is received determine how cash flow is managed. In this chapter we provide brief discussions of the different types of income that can be a part of cash flow in nonprofit organizations. It would be highly unusual for your nonprofit to have every type of income we have identified. Most often organizations count on income from one or several sources to support their operations. Therefore in this chapter we have included references to other chapters in *The Cash Flow Management Book for Nonprofits* to guide you in finding more information about the type of income specific to your organization. At the end of this chapter, there is a quick reference guide listing various types of income and where information related to each one can be found in the book.

Generally, nonprofits either earn income through charging for goods and services or receiving resources (cash and noncash) from government agencies, foundations, businesses, other nonprofits, and private individuals. As stated previously, the type of income and the manner in which it is received will affect virtually every aspect of an organization's financial management system, including:

- Budgeting processes (cash flow forecasting, operational budgeting, departmental budgeting, capital budgeting, and so on)
- General accounting procedures and practices
- Charts of accounts
- Billing and collection procedures
- Bookkeeping and record keeping
- Internal and external reporting
- Internal controls
- IRS return filing and taxation
- Audit requirements
- Cash flow planning and management

In this chapter we identify and discuss the following major topics related to income classification and cash flow:

- Classifying income
- Managing donated income and resources
- Managing earned income
- Managing asset-generated income

A. Classifying Income

One of the basic foundations of this book is that the types of income received by organizations will determine the approaches that should be used in managing cash flow. The Financial Accounting Standards Board (FASB), which is responsible for issuing accounting standards in the United States for nongovernmental entities, has created three classifications for net assets applicable to nonprofit organizations:

- **Unrestricted Net Assets.** These are defined in FASB Statement of Financial Standards No. 116 as "neither permanently restricted nor temporarily restricted by donor-imposed stipulations."

- **Temporarily Restricted Net Assets.** These are assets for which use is limited to specific purposes or time periods, as specified in contracts, grant agreements, or other written or oral statements.

- **Permanently Restricted Net Assets.** These are assets held in perpetuity for a specific purpose (for example, endowments), although the nonprofit can classify income generated from the principal amount as temporarily restricted or unrestricted, depending on donor stipulations. Restrictions on the use of net assets may be conveyed either orally or in writing and may be made:
  1. By the individual or organization providing the resources at the time they are given (known as *donor restrictions*)
  2. As a result of specific statements or commitments made when the organization originally solicited the contribution

Note

State laws differ on the definition of an endowment.

Donor restrictions can only be changed by the organization or individual that made the contribution. Similarly, restrictions placed on contributions by the organization at the time of solicitation may only be changed with the consent of the donor(s). In addition, a nonprofit's board can decide that unrestricted funds may be designated for specific purposes. However, restrictions placed by a board of directors do not change the FASB classification of these funds (termed *board-designated funds*) as unrestricted net assets because the board is free to remove the restrictions at its own discretion.

Contributions that are not specifically designated as temporarily or permanently restricted will be considered unrestricted. Also, the funds received as a result of fundraising campaigns or special events will be considered unrestricted unless the organization had stated that the contribution would be used for a specific purpose when it was solicited. Generally, funds obtained through selling donated or other goods or providing services will be unrestricted unless otherwise stated during sales or solicitation.

Funds provided by government agencies are far more likely to have specific performance requirements than those provided by private individuals or foundations. Although the government has many rules that go along with its funding, such funds are still considered unrestricted net assets by the FASB.

B. Managing Donated Income and Resources

Tax-exempt organizations receive money and other resources in a number of ways and from a number of different sources. The characteristics of each of these income streams will require a somewhat different approach to cash flow planning and management. Several of the major categories of contributed income and resources are:

- Grants of various types and from various sources

- Donations, gifts, and contributions

- Membership dues, assessments, or other payments from members

- Payments made in exchange for the right to attend certain fundraising events (known as *special fundraising income*)

Part Three provides detailed information and strategies on cash flow management and planning for each of these types of income.

1. Grants

a. Conditions of Grant. Nonprofits can receive grants from both private and public sources; in either case, grants are often accompanied by written *grant agreements,* or contracts specifying what the recipient organization must do in return for the funding. The legally binding requirements in most grant agreements (usually known as *conditions of grant*) tend to fall into three broad categories:

1. *Restrictions* on how resources can be used

2. *Compliance requirements,* which require organizations to comply with specific laws, regulations, and practices in any of a wide range of areas (see the subsection titled "Government Grants" later in this chapter for some compliance examples)

3. *Measurable goals or service requirements,* which require nonprofits to achieve specific results or to provide specific quantifiable levels of goods or services to particular groups of individuals (known as *target groups* or *charitable classes*)

Grant agreements can directly (or by reference) require nonprofits to meet a wide range of requirements, including:

- Eligibility standards defining the groups or individuals that must be served under the grant

- Kinds and levels of services or activities the nonprofit must provide

- Additional funds or other resources that must be provided as a matching share to qualify for the grant funds

- Allowable and unallowable expenditures

- Requirements and procedures for making changes in the specific amounts, categories, or line items contained in an approved budget

- Specific hiring, personnel, accounting, cash management, record-keeping, reporting, and auditing requirements

- A wide range of other legally binding requirements that can affect a nonprofit's financial management

Program Matching Shares

Some grants may be accompanied by grant agreements that require, as a condition of grant, that the recipient organization provide a *program matching share*. This type of grant requirement is also referred to as a *match*, a *program match*, or a *matching share*. (Program matching shares should not be confused with challenge grants, which are defined later in this chapter.) The amount of the program matching share required is usually defined as a percentage of the resources the nonprofit needs to operate the specific program or activity. For example, a funding source or donor that requires a 25 percent program matching share is agreeing to provide 75 percent of the resources needed to support a particular program or activity. The organization is responsible for providing the remaining 25 percent.

Conditions of grant are usually subject to audit, either by the specific funding source or as part of the organization's own annual audit. Obviously, specific conditions of grant can directly and indirectly affect almost every aspect of an organization's financial management system. Therefore financial managers must carefully read all grant documents and identify all conditions of grant (especially those affecting financial management and cash flow). Managers may then take whatever actions are needed to ensure that financial and cash flow management systems can and will meet all tracking, accounting, and reporting requirements.

b. Matching Requirements. Funding sources may require organizations to meet program matching requirements through one of three methods:

1. A *cash match*, in which the organization must actually provide a specified amount of matching funds (sometimes limited to funds from certain categories or sources)

2. An *in-kind match*, in which an organization can meet matching requirements by receiving in-kind contributions of rental space, equipment, materials, or services, as long as the fair market value of the in-kind goods or services equals the required matching amount

3. A combined cash and in-kind match

The matching requirements of some types of grants will allow organizations to provide program matching shares simply by allocating existing resources to the required purpose. However, some grant agreements will specify that the organization must acquire new funds or resources. In any event, a program matching share is a condition of grant—a contractual obligation—that the organization agrees to meet at the time it receives the support. To avoid violating the grant agreement, organizations must comply with all matching requirements.

When any funding source requires a matching share, the organization usually must:

- Disclose the planned source(s) and value of the required program matching share in a budget or statement accompanying its initial request for funds

- Document in its financial records how, when, and from what sources the required program matching share was actually provided

In addition, a nonprofit's agreement to provide a program matching share usually becomes an auditable compliance requirement. This means the nonprofit's auditors must determine whether or not the organization actually met the promised program matching requirements and must cite in the audit report any material non-compliance they find.

Challenge Grants

Challenge grants are grants that have, as a condition of grant, special program matching requirements. In a challenge grant situation, a funding source promises to provide an organization with money once the organization has attracted a specific amount of new support from other outside sources. In other words, the funding source promises to "match" the contributions the organization acquires from other sources.

c. Government Grants. Organizations that receive federal funds are subject to requirements beyond those attached to other income streams. Such additional requirements can affect cash flow management, particularly in its reporting and analysis aspects. A number of states have specific rules governing the operation of nonprofit organizations that legally do business in the state or solicit contributions from the state's residents. Depending on the amount of the organization's revenues or assets, states may also require that organizations be audited according to generally accepted auditing standards (GAAS), as issued by the American Institute of Certified Public Accountants (AICPA). Specific funding sources can establish additional audit requirements, which is often the case with federal funds. Receiving federal, state, or local government funds can subject a nonprofit to three sets of auditing requirements in addition to GAAS:

1. The audit requirements set forth in the General Accounting Office's *Government Auditing Standards* (also known as the "Yellow Book")

2. The audit requirements spelled out in Office of Management and Budget Circular A-133 *(Audits of States, Local Governments and Nonprofit Organizations)*

3. Any applicable state, city, or local audit requirements

These three types of audit requirements can affect nonprofit financial and cash flow management in many ways. For example, failure to follow the detailed requirements for record keeping, auditing, and compliance with a wide range of laws and regulations can lead to sanctions, including discontinuation of cash inflow. In this case, cash flow will be restored only when the requirements set forth in your grant agreement are met. Organizations that are subject to Circular A-133 and Yellow Book standards or other federal accounting or oversight regulations must make sure to comply with all requirements and to build all necessary elements into their cash flow planning and management systems. Some of the financial and accounting regulations that are relevant to cash flow management and that also apply to government-funded programs include:

- Allowable costs and cost principles involving direct and indirect costs

- Rules regarding the handling of interest earned on any advances of federal funds

- Rules defining exactly how the organization computes its cash flow needs

- Rules regarding the handling of income generated as a result of program activities

- Rules regarding procurement (bidding and purchasing)

- Rules regarding revolving-fund repayments

- Rules requiring the organization's auditors to meet certain experience and training requirements

- Rules regarding identifying, tracking, and reporting on funds and their use in accordance with the funding source's requirements and as part of completing IRS annual information returns

- Rules mandating the chart of accounts and budget categories by line item that a nonprofit must use in tracking and recording income and expenses

Organizations for which grants are a source of income should refer to Chapters Eight and Fourteen for more detailed discussions of relevant cash flow strategies and information.

2. Gifts and Contributions

Gifts and *contributions* are cash or other assets provided to an organization to support its exempt activities by donors who are eligible to receive little or nothing of direct value in exchange. Gifts and contributions can come from individual, corporate, foundation, or other sources, including bequests. However, if a *tangible benefit* (that is, goods or services) of more than nominal value is offered in return for a contribution, only the amount above the fair market value of the goods or services offered is considered to be a contribution. If the specific individual, group, or organization making a payment is eligible to receive in return direct tangible or economic benefits for which the fair market value equals or exceeds the amount of the payment, none of the payment qualifies as a gift, grant, or contribution. Instead, it may qualify as income from a trade or business.

Donors can place restrictions on how a nonprofit may use gifts or contributions. They can also make pledges of future support that obligate the nonprofit to do certain things within a specified time period in order to receive the resources pledged. (For more information see the subsection titled "Pledges of Future Support" further on in this chapter.)

In order to properly manage cash flow for gift and contribution income, a nonprofit's financial management system must be able to:

- Identify the fair market value of any goods or services offered in return for contributions, membership payments, or admission to special fundraising events

- Identify the expenses involved in generating such payments and determine the total amount of income that qualifies as contributions and that is therefore tax deductible to the donor

- Provide individual donors who make individual contributions of over $250 with written statements regarding the tax deductibility of their donations

- Identify and track individual donations, gifts, and contributions for which use is restricted

Note
An individual could give your organization $1 million to help build a new athletic field. If this money is restricted by the donor, as described earlier, then your organization cannot ethically (or, in many states, legally) use that money to pay staff not associated with the project. Thus effective cash flow management of contributions includes following the rules that govern this distinct income flow.

a. Noncash Contributions. Organizations may receive two types of noncash contributions from individuals, corporations, or other nonprofits:

1. Property (for example, securities, land, facilities, equipment, materials, or supplies)

2. Services or use of equipment, facilities, or materials owned by others when the service or use is provided free or at reduced cost

Receiving noncash contributions in a form the organization can use to fulfill a purpose reduces the need for the organization to spend cash for that purpose. This will obviously help cash flow. When the contribution is of securities of a publicly traded company, the organization can usually sell the security rapidly and have cash available in a short period of time. Organizations need to have cash flow management policies to properly handle such types of contributions.

Nonprofits must be able to identify, track, and report on each of the various sorts of noncash contributions they receive. Information on income from contributions will be necessary for generating financial statements, documenting the contribution in preparation for the annual audit, completing and submitting the required annual IRS information return, and issuing any required state reports.

Organizations for which contributions constitute an income stream should refer to Chapters Eight and Thirteen for relevant cash flow strategies and information.

b. Pledges. *Pledges* are promises to provide future support in the form of cash, securities, land, buildings, use of facilities or utilities, materials, supplies, intangible assets, or services. Pledges can be either conditional or unconditional. *Unconditional pledges* are economic support that donors promise to give with no conditions. *Conditional pledges* are support promised to the nonprofit only if specific conditions are met or come to pass.

Nonprofits must be able to identify, track, and report on individual pledges as either conditional or unconditional. Organizations will have to decide how pledges will be incorporated into cash flow forecasts and make this part of the organization's cash flow policy. If $1 million is pledged for a particular purpose (such as for a new athletic field, to use the example mentioned earlier), that money should not go into cash flow projections until the date that the organization is actually working on planning or building that project.

3. Membership Dues and Assessments

Membership dues or *assessments* are payments that organizations receive from members in exchange for offering them membership privileges. In terms of cash flow management, organizations must be able to perform proper record keeping and reporting when receiving membership dues.

Organizations for which membership dues are a part of cash flow should refer to Chapters Eight and Sixteen for specific cash flow strategies and detailed information.

4. Income from Special Fundraising Events

Specific nonprofit fundraising events or activities constitute a substantial portion of some nonprofits' income. Cash flow planning and management for special-event income will include taking the necessary steps to comply with required Internal Revenue Service and financial reporting. Organizations must have financial and cash flow management systems in place to prepare financial reports required to report fundraising event income by event and in total.

Organizations for which any type of special-event income is a part of their cash flow should refer to Chapters Eight and Seventeen for specific cash flow strategies and detailed information.

C. Managing Earned Income

Tax-exempt nonprofits can earn income by providing goods or services for a fee. "Selling" different kinds of goods and services can generate different kinds of *income,* such as:

- Income from trade or business activities
- Income from sales of assets
- Income from program service fees
- Income from fees paid by government agencies (as opposed to grants or awards)

Each of these ways of earning income is discussed in the following subsections.

1. Income from Trade or Business Activities

Nonprofits are allowed to generate income by carrying out trade or business activities. Such income falls into three basic categories:

1. Related business income: tax-free income from trade or business activities that are "substantially related" to a nonprofit's exempt purpose

2. Unrelated business income (UBI): income from trade or business activities that are "not substantially related" to a nonprofit's exempt purpose

3. Income that would appear to be UBI but that is actually tax free because it is excluded from unrelated business income tax (UBIT) under the Internal Revenue Code or specific legislation

Nonprofits that conduct trade or business activities must be able to identify, track, and report on all related, unrelated, and excluded income (as well as applicable expenses) in order to:

- Determine the actual costs involved in carrying out specific trade or business activities to promote effective cash flow planning and management
- Prepare accurate financial statements
- Meet audit requirements successfully
- Classify and report income correctly on their annual IRS information return

• Determine whether they must file IRS Form 990-T (Exempt-Organization Business Income Tax Return) and calculate how much estimated UBIT, if any, they must pay

Organizations that might be subject to UBIT should refer to Chapter Eight, Section I, for information about UBIT.

2. Income from Sales of Assets

Nonprofits must be able to track income gains or losses from assets they sell. However, different types of assets are subject to different UBIT treatment and IRS reporting requirements. For example, to complete IRS Form 990 (Return of Organization Exempt from Income Tax), a nonprofit must be able to identify, track, account for, and report separately on income from the sale of at least three different kinds of assets:

1. Income from selling property held as part of a trade or business activity

2. Capital gains from selling investments or other noninventory property (that is, property not intended for sale as part of a trade or business)

3. Income from selling real or personal property that was donated within the prior two years and for which the donor claimed a federal income tax deduction

Not only must income from the sale of each kind of asset be reported separately on Form 990, but some of the income may be subject to UBIT, some may be completely tax free, and still other income may be excluded from UBIT under specific sections of the Internal Revenue Code. UBIT liability, as well as the multiple record-keeping and reporting requirements, will have an impact on cash flow planning and management for organizations that benefit from this type of income stream.

Organizations for which the sales of assets constitute an aspect of cash flow should refer to Chapters Eight, Twelve, and Nineteen for specific cash flow strategies and more detailed information.

3. Income from Program Service Fees

A nonprofit can charge fees for services it provides—services that can be either related or unrelated to the organization's exempt purpose. Organizations may receive fees for services directly from the individuals or organizations they serve, from third parties who agree to pay all or some of the fees, or from some combination of the two.

When an organization generates fees for services, its financial management system must be able to generate bills and record collections for individual accounts and to track associated income and expenses.

Program service income (also called *fee-for-service income*) is primarily income a nonprofit receives in exchange for providing goods or services that further its exempt purpose. Program service revenue can include income from related trade or business activities as well as fees for other services.

Program service income will require organizations to develop financial management systems that are capable of performing all of the necessary billing, collection, data management, reporting, and analysis functions. This type of income stream can be one of the most complex in terms of cash flow planning and management.

Organizations that receive program service income should refer to Chapters Eight and Eleven for specific cash flow strategies and more detailed information.

4. Income from Fees Paid by Government Agencies

A nonprofit can receive fees from a government agency for providing goods or services to the agency. Fees from government agencies only include payments for services, facilities, or products that primarily benefit the government agency, either economically or physically. They do not include government grants or other payments that help a nonprofit provide services or maintain facilities for direct public benefit.

Service Agreements

Nonprofits may enter into contracts with private and public entities, such as individuals, governmental units, or other nonprofits, to provide services in exchange for money (these are known as *service agreements, service contracts,* or *performance contracts*). Such agreements may supply a nonprofit with agreed-on resources either before or after the nonprofit has provided specified goods or services. Under such contracts the resources supplied are often determined by the specific amount of services the nonprofit provides. For example, Universal Nonprofit has a program that offers comprehensive mental health counseling services to the community. To derive the greatest benefit from the staff and structure of this program, Universal Nonprofit has also negotiated service contracts with other organizations to provide their staffs with employee assistance program services for a fee.

As with grant agreements, any contract can directly (or by reference) commit the nonprofit to meet a wide range of requirements, including standards for eligibility, levels of service, matching resources, accounting, auditing, reporting, and expenditures, as well as other legally binding requirements that can affect a nonprofit's financial management. Some of these legally binding requirements may be restrictions on how resources can be used. Other requirements (*compliance requirements*) may bind the organization to comply with specific laws, regulations, and practices governing hiring, accounting, record keeping, cash management, and so on. Still other requirements may obligate the nonprofit to provide specific levels of goods or services to particular groups of individuals (*target populations* or *charitable classes*). Obviously, a nonprofit's financial management system must be able to identify, track, account for, and report on all income and compliance requirements accompanying a contract.

D. Managing Asset-Generated Income

Tax-exempt nonprofits can earn income by using existing assets to produce income, usually through investments. This is because nonprofits are generally allowed to invest money and engage in the same sorts of investment transactions as for-profit entities. In addition to cash investments, such as interest-bearing bank accounts and certificates of deposit (CDs), a nonprofit's investments can also include any noninventory property (that is, property not intended for sale as part of a trade or business), such as stocks, bonds, options to purchase or sell securities, and real estate.

Note

Some state laws prohibit using endowment funds for certain investments.

Categories of asset-generated income that affect nonprofit financial management, and therefore may require special cash flow management, include:

- Income from debt-financed assets
- Interest income
- Dividend income
- Gains or losses on investment transactions
- Gains or losses on disposition of assets
- Endowment income
- Rental income from real or personal property
- Royalty income
- Income a nonprofit "parent" receives from a "controlled" taxable subsidiary

Asset-generated income from any of these sources will have financial and cash flow planning and management requirements that are specific to the source, amount, and restriction status of the assets involved. Also, there will be requirements based on whether or not the income is related to the organization's tax-exempt purpose.

In the majority of cases each type of asset will require separate treatment, both in terms of cash flow planning and management and in terms of general accounting and reporting. Generally, the cash flow difference between asset-generated income and other income streams is that there will be fewer expenses and very little labor involved in receiving the income. This factor, as well as the often greater record-keeping, reporting, accounting, and tax considerations for asset-generated income, will have a substantial effect on cash flow planning and management.

Because each type of asset-generated income is unique in its cash flow considerations, we have not distinguished them in detail in this section. We cover different types of asset-generated income individually in Part Three.

Organizations for which interest, dividend, or royalty income is a source of cash flow should refer to Chapters Eight and Fifteen for specific cash flow strategies and detailed information. Organizations that receive rental income should refer to Chapter Eighteen for further information and cash flow strategies.

E. Which Chapters in This Book Are Most Relevant to Your Organization?

Not every organization will derive revenue from every source we cover in this book, so not every chapter of this book will be applicable to every reader. We have included a quick reference guide (Exhibit 2.1) to help you use *The Cash Flow Management Book for Nonprofits,* based on your organization's revenue streams and the information you are likely to find useful.

Exhibit 2.1 lists possible revenue streams and the chapter numbers of each chapter in this book. To determine which chapters will be most useful to you, locate in the leftmost column of Exhibit 2.1 each revenue stream applicable to your organization and read across to see which chapters are checkmarked.

EXHIBIT 2.1 Quick Reference Guide to the Chapters in This Book

REVENUE STREAM OF YOUR ORGANIZATION

CHAPTER

REVENUE STREAM OF YOUR ORGANIZATION	1	2	3	4	5	6	7	8	9	10	11	12	13	14	15	16	17	18	19	20	21
Program Services	✓	✓	✓	✓	✓	✓	✓	✓	✓	✓	✓									✓	✓
Grants	✓	✓	✓	✓	✓	✓	✓	✓	✓	✓				✓						✓	✓
Membership Dues	✓	✓	✓	✓	✓	✓	✓	✓		✓						✓				✓	✓
Real Estate or Rentals	✓	✓	✓	✓	✓	✓	✓	✓		✓								✓		✓	✓
Investments	✓	✓	✓	✓	✓	✓	✓	✓		✓					✓					✓	✓
Contributions	✓	✓	✓	✓	✓	✓	✓	✓		✓			✓						✓	✓	✓
Inventory	✓	✓	✓	✓	✓	✓	✓	✓		✓		✓								✓	✓
Special Events	✓	✓	✓	✓	✓	✓	✓	✓		✓							✓			✓	✓
Sales of Assets	✓	✓	✓	✓	✓	✓	✓	✓		✓									✓	✓	✓
Interest, Dividends, or Royalties	✓		✓	✓	✓	✓	✓	✓		✓					✓					✓	✓
Capital Projects	✓	✓	✓	✓	✓	✓	✓	✓	✓	✓										✓	✓

CHAPTER 3
Cash Flow Management and Internal Controls: An Overview

An essential component of effective cash flow management is a system of internal controls. Internal controls consist of documented policies and procedures designed to protect your organization's assets. It is not enough for your organization to have an internal-control system in place. Staff must be properly trained in internal-control procedures, and proper supervision and monitoring are necessary to ensure effective functioning of internal controls. Control procedures related to cash management are extremely important, as this aspect of operations is particularly vulnerable to fraud, theft, and errors. To reduce the risk of internal-control failures, cash-related internal controls should be documented by the organization, proper training should be given to staff to ensure a clear understanding and proper implementation of internal control procedures, and ongoing supervision and internal-control monitoring should be performed on a regular basis. The discussion that follows in this chapter is intended as a brief overview of the topic.

We strongly suggest that when designing a system of cash-related internal-control procedures, organizations consult their auditors for guidance. Poorly designed, misunderstood, or inadequately performed internal-control procedures can lead to embezzlement, large losses of inventory, theft, and other types of fraud and error. For example, recently we were engaged by an agency in which the internal-control weaknesses allowed a bookkeeper to steal $50,000. The bookkeeper was able to perpetrate this crime because she was responsible for both preparing checks for issuance and performing the agency's bank reconciliations. Control failures like this one can have a substantial impact on cash flow, so internal control is much more than just an intellectual concept. In the agency just described, the control failure resulted in a 10 percent loss of net worth, not to mention embarrassment for management and the board of directors. The agency suffered a reduction in confidence, morale, and image, both internally and externally.

A. The Control Environment

Spending the proper amount of time and money to prevent control failures is very cheap insurance against loss from fraud, theft, and error. Developing a secure operating environment requires that a comprehensive, practical, and integrated internal-control structure be in place to protect *all* vulnerable operations and functions, not just cash flow. Creating this structure, even though it is essential to the financial health of organizations, is beyond the scope of this book. However, many of the general concepts we discuss may also be applied to improve internal control throughout your organization. Segregation of duties, active and responsible management, and ongoing monitoring of internal controls will benefit every aspect of the control environment, which will ultimately enhance cash flow.

In this chapter we offer suggestions for establishing an effective internal-control system related to cash flow management. The strategies described in this chapter are those that most affect cash flow.

B. Cash Receipts

The cash receipt cycle is one of the most sensitive segments of the accounting process. Management must ensure that employees have as little access to cash as possible. Employees should only have access to cash or the ability to process cash receipts if these tasks are a necessary part of performing their jobs or fulfilling the requirements of their positions. Reducing the number of employees with access to cash will reduce the chances of cash receipt mistakes and theft.

However, the need to limit employee access to cash must also be balanced with the need to provide adequate controls. A checks-and-balances system should be in place so that no single person is responsible for all aspects of a transaction. For example, if one staff member opens the mail and enters the cash-related data into the record-keeping system, another staff member should prepare the deposit slip and deposit the money. Ideally, a third staff member will review the transaction. Small nonprofits may not have three staff members in their finance department, so alternative methods to protect smaller organizations must be designed. For example, some small organizations may have board members and auditors help monitor financial records.

The structure of the cash receipt cycle will also determine the risk of fraud. For example, if the cash receipt cycle primarily involves mail receipts, it is more risky than a cash receipt cycle that uses lockbox services. In using bank lockbox services, the organization relies on the bank's control structure to ensure that cash receipts are deposited and recorded. The organization does not have to participate in the control system because the person writing the check sends the money directly to the bank. Another useful cash receipt control procedure is to have an employee without access to cash or accounts receivable compare cash receipts with validated deposit slips. Endorsing all checks immediately upon receipt as "for deposit only" with the account number of the organization is also a practical and easy-to-implement safeguard. This endorsement makes it difficult for the depositor to receive cash for the deposit.

One of the most important aspects of a successful cash management process is instituting procedures to ensure that cash is deposited as quickly as possible. Preferably, all cash receipts will be deposited at the end of each day. This will allow the organization to maintain the largest cash balance possible at any given point in time. It will also help deter fraud by reducing opportunities for theft.

Special-event cash receipts must be treated with particular vigilance. The fact that special events are not frequent activities and that they usually involve more people makes these income-generating activities especially vulnerable. Organizations must take special precautions to ensure that they do not lose income from events through control failures. For example, volunteers who collect money from special-event sales should not also be responsible for monitoring and recording the organization's cash receipts.

Another method for reducing the risk of cash loss due to control failure is to use prenumbered cash receipts. These will deter theft of funds, as management will be able to isolate missing cash receipts more quickly and efficiently. The best advice regarding special-event internal control is to find an experienced veteran of special-event programs and coordinate a planning meeting with your auditor to brainstorm how to protect your special event. One strategy used by many organizations is to design the event so that absolutely no cash is collected at the event itself. All donations, fees, and "silent auction" or other activity funds can be collected by check before the event or after the event.

C. Receivables

The internal controls for receivables (such as grants receivable or funds due from other funding sources) will concern maintaining adequate controls over receipt and management. As with the internal-control system for other areas of operation, more than one person, but as few as possible, should be involved in the receipt and management of receivables. The danger in just a single staff member being responsible for receivables is that the employee might be able to steal receipts and then eliminate the accounts receivable records without being detected. An internal-control environment that contains adequate checks and balances will reduce the occurrence of this type of fraud. People can be very creative when trying to steal money. We have heard of employees who set up bank accounts with names similar to their employers' names and then used the accounts for deposit and theft of corporate funds.

D. Cash Disbursements

The organization must also design internal controls to guard against mistakes and fraud in the cash disbursement cycle. The organization must limit access to the means by which cash is disbursed and to all cash disbursement records. The fewer staff members who are involved in disbursement-related record keeping (above the number necessary to ensure checks and balances), the lower the risk of error and fraud. The following are some suggestions for developing internal controls related to cash disbursement procedures:

1. *Cash disbursements should be made by check.* Using checks for disbursement adds an automatic layer of control to every transaction. When cash disbursements must be made in the form of cash, they should be substantiated by written authorization and by receipts documenting the transaction.

2. *Checks should be disbursed in numerical order.* Voided checks (with records documenting the reason they were voided) should be the only interruption in the continuous sequence of check numbers. Blank checks should be inspected on a periodic basis to ensure that all blank checks are present and accounted for. A staff member or small group should be given direct responsibility for the security of blank checks. Blank checks should be kept in a locked and secured location at all times.

3. *Procedures for check preparation and check signing should require a clear separation of duties different people should perform.* Although these two operations will be functionally linked, they must remain separate to preserve the integrity of the internal-control structure. An employee who is independent of the payment approval process should handle the check preparation. The check preparer should examine all supporting documentation for legitimacy, reasonableness, and proper approvals. Cash disbursements should only be issued on vendor invoices and not on account statements. Furthermore, when checks are made out, they should be written to a specific named party and never to "Cash" or "Bearer." If a check is for petty cash purposes, it should be made out in the name of the petty cash custodian. All supporting documentation should accompany the prepared check as it is forwarded to the appropriate person for signature.

4. *Check-signing procedures should focus more on who is signing than on what is being signed.* Check signing is the final procedure in the cash disbursement cycle. The check preparation phase should catch any fraudulent transactions. As a final safeguard, those with signatory authority should review all supporting material. Checks should only be signed by a person who has board authorization to perform this function. Transactions over certain predetermined dollar amount should require that a second person countersign the check. For every transaction the authorized check signer should be independent of the procedures for payment approval, check preparation, and purchasing, and (when checks involve payroll functions) time records. The objective in maintaining these procedures is to ensure that only individuals who are responsible and capable sign checks.

5. *Checks should not be signed using a rubber stamp in place of an actual signature, nor should blank checks ever be signed.* We recommend that whenever possible and practical, board members sign all or at least some of the organization's checks. If your organization uses a check signing machine, proper written logs of the use of the device must be maintained.

Note

On more than one occasion in our experience, we have determined that individuals signing checks were legally blind yet were assigned check-signing duties because they held the position of treasurer of the organization. Common sense should always be operative—people signing checks should have the training and capacity to perform their duties.

We recommend, as an additional internal control, that all employees be required to take a vacation. Although this sounds simplistic, we have found this to be an excellent strategy for uncovering control problems. In performing a vacationing employee's job functions, the substitute employee will be able to determine whether or not proper control procedures are being followed.

One of the most important aspects of internal control over cash is the final step in the cycle: performing bank reconciliations. Bank reconciliations should be done as soon as bank statements are received by your organization to ensure that the other aspects of your control structure are effective. A staff member who is removed from both the cash receipt and disbursement processes and who is available to work promptly and with accuracy should be preparing the bank reconciliations. Any errors must be discussed with the individuals responsible for the errors. Corrective action plans should be created if an error appears to be a result of a flaw in the design of the control system.

E. Petty Cash

Organizations that must use petty cash should attempt to do so as little as possible. Petty cash is especially vulnerable to internal-control failures because it is an asset already in its most liquid form. All the review, documentation, and authorization procedures required for cash disbursements should also be performed for replenishment of petty cash funds.

The custodial responsibility for petty cash should be assigned to a minimum of staff members, ideally one or two. Some organizations maintain control over petty cash by limiting the fund to $100 and setting the maximum petty cash reimbursement amount at $20. No matter what the amounts, the custodian of the account should have no access to accounting records and should be independent of the employees who handle cash receipts.

A petty cash voucher system should be developed to ensure that proper documentation exists for each cash disbursement from the petty cash fund. The vouchers should appear in sequential order using a prenumbered format. Each voucher should clearly indicate what the disbursement was for and how much was paid. No voucher should ever be issued for payment without proper documentation.

The petty cash custodian should review all reimbursements made and determine whether or not reimbursements meet the expense criteria of being reasonable and necessary. The petty cash vouchers should be canceled immediately following the issuance of the funds to ensure that the claim is not paid twice. Finally, petty cash should be counted periodically by a person independent of the custodian.

F. Bonding

In order to protect your organization against embezzlement, proper bonding insurance should be purchased. Bonding protects organizations against loss of funds due to theft. In many situations, including one that befell Universal Nonprofit, having adequate bonding insurance allows organizations to recoup losses that occur as a result of embezzlement or theft. In the case of Universal Nonprofit's embezzlement claim, the organization was reimbursed in full for funds lost as a result of poor bank reconciliation procedures. The funds were taken over a three-year period in amounts that were small enough that the organization did not feel an immediate economic impact. Nevertheless, the loss added up to $50,000. Appropriate bonding insurance is an important aspect of any organization's internal-control system.

G. Investments

The internal-control system for investments should be structured to safeguard the bond or stock certificates and other primary documentation that provides evidence of ownership. We recommend that stock certificates or bonds indicating ownership of investments always be held at an established brokerage company. We do not recommend keeping such documents stored in a bank safe-deposit box, unless they are deeds for property. In addition, original documents substantiating ownership of investments should never be stored in-house.

Internal control pertaining to investments must start with investment policies set forth by the board. Such policies should detail investment procedures that must be followed and should include internal controls for managing the invested assets. (For more information on policies regarding investments, see Chapters Two, Four, Eight, Fifteen, and Nineteen.)

H. Payroll

The most important internal-control policy for payroll functions is establishing that staff members who have the authority to set up new employee files are not the same as those who prepare the actual payrolls. One way of ensuring this segregation of functions is structuring the human resources department and the payroll department as two separate and distinct entities. This segregation will reduce the risk of someone creating a "ghost employee" to whom fraudulent payments could be issued. Another strategy for increasing payroll internal control is instituting a policy that requires the passwords used to access personnel and payroll data be changed regularly. Unfortunately, many organizations overlook these fairly simple internal-control mechanisms and suffer substantial losses that might easily have been prevented.

I. Inventory

Organizations that maintain significant inventory must safeguard these assets against loss. Periodic inventory counts should be made to ensure that the accounting records agree with the physical status of the inventory. Also, the organization should review the inventory it is holding for any possible write-downs. (A *write-down* is a reduction of the value of inventory shown in the organization's records.) Organizations should never allow the same staff member to order, receive, and record the transactions associated with inventory.

Some organizations that have substantial inventory may also be selling inventory over a counter in a store, via a catalogue, or via the Internet. Therefore your organization may need specialized software to properly monitor internal control related to sales of inventory. (For more information on managing inventory, see Chapters Ten and Twelve.)

J. Property and Equipment

Internal controls must be developed regarding the purchase of property and equipment. A senior executive should be required to approve all purchases over a certain dollar amount. A second senior employee should review purchase transactions after delivery or installation to ensure that the product ordered was actually the product delivered or installed. Accurate records must be kept regarding the purchase, history, and disposition of all items of equipment to document any insurance claims and to protect equipment from theft. In addition, organizations should have systems in place to oversee large maintenance or repair contracts. Unfortunately, kickback schemes, in which contractors perform shoddy, incomplete, or completely bogus work, are not uncommon.

Using Policies, Forecasts, Budgets, Strategies, and Technology to Improve Cash Flow Management

PART TWO CONTAINS information and instructions on improving overall cash flow planning and management and on increasing income. This section of the book includes chapters on policy and procedure development, operating budgets, cash flow forecasting, cash flow monitoring, reporting, and analysis, cash flow improvement strategies, cash flow planning for capital projects, and the use of technology in cash flow management.

CHAPTER 4
Cash Flow Policy and Procedure Development

Organizations that would like to optimize cash flow must have written policies and procedures in place to guide cash flow planning and management. Lack of policies, poorly developed policies, and ignored policies are common causes of cash flow problems. Organizations should make the development of cash flow planning and management policies a top priority. Unfortunately, Universal Nonprofit had not. Indeed, many of Universal Nonprofit's cash flow problems could ultimately be traced back to a lack of effective policies and procedures related to cash flow management. Therefore developing policies and procedures was one of the first steps in helping Universal Nonprofit improve cash flow.

Ideally, policy and procedure development should involve a team representing every operational division that will be involved in cash flow management. In this chapter we offer suggestions on basic policy development, on what must be included in written policies and procedural guidelines, and on the types of policies that will be helpful in planning and managing cash flow.

A. General Guidelines for Policy Development

Developing written policies is an important step in improving any aspect of operations. Thus it should be undertaken with care, forethought, research, structure, and input from a broad constituency within and outside the organization (including auditors, funding sources, banks, and so on). Keep in mind that these policies will be used on a regular basis and that "doing it right the first time" will save time and money. All written policy development should incorporate the following elements:

- Input from those who will have to implement the policy and from those whom the policy will affect

- Thorough step-by-step review of existing written (or formal) and unwritten (or informal) policies and procedures that relate to those being developed

- Assessment of existing policies to determine which are effective and should be preserved, which need modification, and which should be eliminated

- Review of planned activities to assess whether or not new policies will be needed

- Review of the draft copy of the new policies by those who will be responsible for implementation and those who will be affected by the new policies

- Staff orientations to familiarize all relevant personnel with the new policies once they are finalized and to provide a forum for questions and answers

B. Characteristics of Effective Policies

Having policies that are difficult to understand or that are missing essential information is almost worse than having no written policies at all. Policies should be well organized and concise. The individuals who are writing the policies must have a good understanding of both the subject matter and the best way to implement the policies. Organizations that are rewriting or initially developing policies and procedures should always create a calendar or schedule. This calendar will list all of the tasks in policy development, such as the ones identified in the preceding section. The calendar should also identify who will be responsible for completing the tasks, what each task will involve, and the due date for each task.

Generally, a written policy should designate or include:

- The name of the policy and a short description of its purpose

- The scope of the policy, including the circumstances, transactions, decisions, and staff members to which the policy applies

- Those responsible for writing the policy

- Those responsible for preapproval review or input regarding the policy, such as:

  1. Outside funding sources that require specific actions or procedures in the given policy area (such as purchasing of certain kinds or amounts of equipment)
  2. The corporate attorney (for policies involving legal questions or requiring a legal opinion)
  3. The independent auditor (for policies involving government cost principles, special regulatory rules, tax issues, or other auditing requirements)
  4. The board (usually its review and input are required before it exercises its final approval authority)
  5. Employees and organizational units that will be most affected by the policy

- Those responsible for communicating the policy to others and interpreting it

- Those responsible for ensuring compliance with the policy on the part of specific people or units

- Those responsible for reviewing and updating the policy and its related procedures

- Those responsible for changing actual day-to-day procedures to ensure compliance with the policy

- Those responsible for carrying out each element of the policy

- The timetable for implementing each element of the policy

- Any checks and balances, supervision, or approval necessary in order to implement the policy

- Any reporting or record-keeping requirements relevant to implementing the policy

- Procedures for modifying the policy, including who may modify it and under what circumstances, as well as what processes and approvals are necessary in order to modify it

- Procedures for overriding the policy, including who may override it and under what circumstances, as well as what processes and approvals are necessary in order to override it

Reporting and Record-Keeping Requirements

Reporting and record-keeping requirements constitute an especially important aspect of policy development when reporting involves requirements imposed by funding sources or regulatory bodies. The part of a written policy that addresses reporting and record-keeping requirements should include the following items: the nature of the reporting, who is responsible for preparing reports, to whom the reports must be submitted, what will be done with the reported information, and what actions will be taken to address the results of any analyses done on the reported information. For all of these items, the policy should designate the relevant time frames, the responsible parties, and any supervision or approval necessary.

C. Policies Related to Cash Flow Planning and Management

Many organizational policies will in some way relate to cash flow. However, overall financial policy development is beyond the scope of this book. The following list of policies include those we believe are directly relevant and necessary to effective cash flow planning and management. Policies are needed for:

- Establishing the frequency of preparation and the format of cash flow forecasts, reports, and analyses, including who is responsible for preparing these documents and to whom they will be disseminated

- Establishing all billing and collection procedures

- Establishing investment procedures, including acceptable investment types and returns

- Establishing banking procedures, including who may authorize bank loans

- Identifying what actions will be taken, and by whom, to address short- and long-term negative cash flow situations

- Projecting income, including the certainty or uncertainty of receiving future income
- Projecting cash inflow and outflow
- Establishing internal controls related to cash management, including fraud prevention measures
- Establishing procedures and responsibilities regarding application for new funding
- Establishing procedures for modification of existing cash flow forecasts
- Establishing a methodology for planning and implementing capital campaigns
- Establishing guidelines for managing endowments
- Establishing proper levels of working capital
- Identifying actions to be taken to collect accounts receivable
- Identifying actions to be taken for past due accounts receivable
- Establishing dollar amount thresholds at which specific executive or board approvals will be required for purchases (creating a "table of authorities")
- Establishing bidding and other negotiation procedures to be used with suppliers and vendors
- Establishing the board's role in cash flow planning and management
- Establishing the internal flow of cash flow management information
- Identifying the level of certainty needed to include anticipated funds in cash flow forecasts
- Establishing procedures for making decisions about whether to purchase or lease property, equipment, and so on
- Establishing guidelines for processing and managing income from special events, related business activities, and unrelated business activities

Operating Budgets in Cash Flow Management

Effective operating budgets are the starting point in planning and managing cash flow. When operating budgets are not properly developed—when they do not reflect reality or are otherwise inaccurate—they make effective cash flow management impossible. *The Budget-Building Book for Nonprofits* (by Murray Dropkin and Bill La Touche; Jossey-Bass, 1998) provides specific instruction on how to develop budgeting processes that result in effective operating budgets.

A. Operating Budgets: Basic Concepts

Keep in mind while reading this chapter that operational budgeting is based on *accrual-basis accounting*. Using an accrual basis means that items are shown as income for a fiscal period even though they were not actually received in that fiscal period—as long as they were earned during that period and legally belong to the organization. The money not yet received yet already earned is a *receivable*. (We discuss this and other differences between operational budgeting and cash flow forecasting in greater detail in Chapter Six.) Similarly, in an accrual-basis accounting system, items of expense are shown as expenses for a fiscal period even when they are not actually paid for during that fiscal period. Those items not paid for but still shown as expenses are referred to as *accounts payable, accrued expenses,* or by other names, depending on the organization.

There is one major conceptual difference between operational budgeting and cash flow forecasting. Unlike operational budgeting, cash flow forecasting is based on *cash-basis accounting,* which only recognizes cash actually received and cash actually paid out. The reason cash flow forecasting uses cash-basis accounting is that this concept more accurately reflects the organization's cash position.

For example, the CFO of your organization could tell you that your organization has a $1 million excess of income versus expenses on your organization's accrual-basis financial statements. In the next breath the CFO could tell you that your organization will not be able to pay next week's payroll. Both statements can be true at the same time. Perhaps a major funding source owes your organization a large amount of money. Legally, you earned the money by fulfilling the requirements of your grant or contract, so the money would be included in accrual-based financial reports. However, the fact that the money is not yet in your organization's bank account is the only one relevant in terms of cash flow forecasting.

Developing operating budgets is not a topic that can be adequately covered in one chapter. Indeed, whole volumes have been devoted to helping organizations perform this most important task (including *The Budget-Building Book for Nonprofits*). However, as a refresher, in the remainder of this chapter we have summarized some major aspects of developing operating budgets. The following sections include:

- An overview of budgeting

- An introduction to some budget-building strategies

- An explanation of how to create a budgeting calendar

- A discussion of how to develop budgeting goals, guidelines, policies, and procedures

B. Overview of Budgeting

If we were limited to making only three overriding statements about the operational-budgeting process, they would be the following:

1. The budget must be based on a sound and clearly defined strategic plan.

2. The budgeting process must involve extensive collaboration.

3. The budget must be monitored on an ongoing basis.

In the area of collaboration, budgeting should be inclusive, bringing together the perspectives and interests of a wide variety of groups: the board, clients, management and staff, prospective donors and income sources, and (when applicable) the general public. At the outset of the budget process, input from all relevant parties should be sought. The approved budget should clearly and effectively communicate to the entire organization the priorities, goals, and operational plans that will advance the underlying strategic plan.

Budgeting as a dynamic process is also an important concept. Budgeting should not occur in a vacuum or for a limited period, producing a document that is never used effectively. Ongoing monitoring, data gathering and analysis, revised budgets and assumptions, and consideration of alternatives are needed.

1. Functions of Nonprofit Budgeting

Budgeting performs a number of important functions. Effective budgeting helps an organization to:

- Adjust plans, activities, and spending as needed

- Spend money cost-effectively

- Reach specific financial goals

- Prevent adverse audit findings

- Avoid incurring disallowed costs or other unnecessary expenses

- Execute good cash flow management

The clearer, more accurate, and more well thought out a budget is in the beginning, the more likely it is that the budget will successfully perform these functions.

Well-prepared budgets have other benefits too. They let everyone in the organization know:

- The goals to be achieved

- The work to be done to reach the goals

- The resources (people and things) needed to get the work done

- The resources available for getting the work done

- The timetable and deadlines for getting specific work done

- The individuals responsible and accountable for doing the required work

Additional functions that budgets serve for well-managed nonprofits include the following:

- Budgets provide the financial and operational guidance needed to successfully implement board policies and directives.

- Budgets allow management to measure and guide the nonprofit's immediate and long-term financial health and operational effectiveness.

- Budgets guide a nonprofit's acquisition and use of resources.

- Budgets anticipate expenses and identify income to pay for those expenses.

- Budgets are tools for controlling spending and avoiding deficits.

- Budgets help integrate administrative, staff, and operating activities.

- Budgets allow management to monitor actual income and expenses against those that were budgeted in order to assess the nonprofit's overall financial situation and alter plans as needed.

- Budgets can serve as the basis for performance reviews and, in some cases, as compensation criteria.

2. Roles and Responsibilities in Nonprofit Budgeting

The roles people play in budgeting generally depend on a nonprofit's size, structure, and income sources. In general, budgets are best developed collaboratively, using the skills and knowledge of those involved at a number of levels. However, because creating a budget may involve sensitive or confidential issues, individuals involved in the budgeting process need to know what is expected of them.

The following descriptions identify the roles people in various positions in the organization may play in the budgeting process. Budgeting roles and responsibilities should be spelled out in written budgeting policies and procedures, which should be kept up to date and must be understood by those involved.

a. The Board of Directors. The board's role can vary according to its members' willingness and ability to commit time and effort to budgeting. Some boards are deeply involved and participate in planning the annual budget strategy and guidelines, draft budget analysis, and final approval. Other boards may rely more on management, effectively restricting the board's role in budgeting to budget review and approval. In addition, boards may designate a finance or budget committee with the specific responsibility of building the budget and monitoring performance against it.

Overall, the board is legally responsible for ensuring that budgets meet applicable laws and regulations, are fiscally sound, and further the nonprofit's tax-exempt purpose. Fulfilling this role generally involves:

- Developing and reviewing the nonprofit's mission statement and its specific goals and activities for achieving the mission

- Creating a statement of strategic program and service priorities to guide decisions about resource allocation during the budget process

- Establishing general budget policies, such as:
  1. Requirements for a balanced budget
  2. Policies on the use of cash reserves
  3. Decisions about salary increases, hiring, layoffs, new programs, capital projects, and major fundraising efforts or capital campaigns

- Reviewing and formally approving the budget

- Reviewing financial and narrative reports on budget implementation on a regular basis and planning for any needed corrective action

Note

If possible, the board's review of budget reports should include a comparison against external or competitive benchmarks. For example, a child-care organization would want to ascertain how much it costs similar organizations to feed a child in day care for one week to determine the accuracy of this budgeted item.

b. The Executive Director or CEO. The executive director (ED) or CEO plays a sustained role in the budgeting process, usually being responsible for:

- Arranging and staffing any early strategic planning sessions with the board

- Preparing options and recommendations to guide budget development

- Ensuring that the budgeting schedule is met

- Reviewing draft budgets and making decisions regarding resource allocation

- Presenting the recommended budget to the board, explaining its provisions and possible consequences, and answering the board's questions

Depending on the size of the nonprofit and its staff, the ED or CEO may delegate many budgeting tasks to the CFO or other managers. However, the CEO always is responsible for ensuring that the budget is accurate, that it adheres to board policies, and that it is submitted on time for board review and approval. The ED or CEO is ultimately responsible for the organization's achievement of budgeted goals.

Once the budget has been approved, the ED or CEO is responsible for working with the CFO to implement it, which involves:

- Communicating the approved budget to management and line staff so they understand it clearly

- Monitoring financial operations on an ongoing basis to compare actual income and expenses to those budgeted

- Identifying negative or positive deviations from the budget and determining what caused the variances

- Recommending or reviewing action plans to correct negative deviations and to capitalize on positive deviations

Finally, the ED or CEO is responsible for communicating the results of financial monitoring and corrective action to the board and seeking its input and approval for needed fiscal or program changes.

c. The CFO. The CFO also plays a major and sustained role, often having day-to day responsibility for coordinating budget development, implementation, and monitoring. Typically, the CFO:

- Creates a budget development calendar and ensures that deadlines are met

- Communicates budgeting policies and procedures to managers and line staff

- Establishes a format for draft budgets

- Develops income and expense forecasts based on reviews of external economic and competitive trends when applicable

- Collaborates in setting expense and income targets in line with strategic plans for programs or units

- Evaluates draft budgets from program or unit managers for accuracy, reasonableness, adherence to applicable guidelines, and availability of anticipated resources

- Discusses draft budgets with the CEO and other managers as needed

- Makes recommendations for reducing, increasing, or reallocating requested resources

- Prepares the budget document, in some cases helping present it to the board once the CEO's budget decisions are made

Often, after the budget is approved, the CFO is responsible for implementing financial reporting and monitoring, including preparing and analyzing budgeted versus actual income and expense reports for management and board use and overseeing any corrective actions needed.

d. Program, Unit, or Activity Managers. The proactive involvement of program, unit, or activity managers is essential to developing budgets that accurately reflect reality. Program managers are often the most knowledgeable on current program needs and the costs and effects of reducing or expanding operations. Program managers may also be able to supply the most relevant information when nonprofits are developing budgets for new programs or activities.

Ideally, program and unit managers are responsible for developing draft budgets for their areas, which can involve consulting other staff to evaluate current or new programs, operating costs, and staff and equipment needs. When it comes to carrying out budgets, program and unit managers often are in the best position to make decisions about resource allocation or recommend changes in activities to meet budgeted expense or income targets. All too frequently, organizations overlook the importance of input from program or unit managers and do not include them in the budgeting team.

Program or unit managers may also be responsible for assessing the costs of continuing or expanding current programs, as well as creating new programs or making modifications to conform to budget policies. In addition, they may meet with the CFO or CEO to review draft budgets and explore options for change. This is a very important step in the budgeting process for future cash flow planning, as reviewing actual performance will give managers an opportunity to assess the accuracy of their ideas and modify cash flow planning accordingly.

After the CFO informs program and unit managers about approved program budgets, they in turn inform staff about any budget or operational changes. They also review regular financial reports in the format set by the CFO, monitor income and expenses, and help develop and implement corrective action plans for their specific areas of responsibility.

e. Other Possible Participants. Depending on the nature of the organization and its management style, a number of others may be involved in budgeting, including:

- *Clerical support staff,* who must prepare various documents and materials throughout the budgeting process and who need to understand the tasks required of them

- *Consultants and outside specialists,* such as independent auditors and accountants, architects, engineers, bond counsel, and specialists in program areas, who also need to know their roles and assignments

- *Selected clients and volunteers,* who often can provide beneficial ideas and input to improve budgets (and whose involvement or budget approval may be required by certain funding sources)

- *Information systems staff,* who may be called on to prepare special reports or otherwise analyze, provide, or integrate data

C. Budgeting Strategies

Effective budget development depends on having clearly defined strategies for the budgeting process. Nonprofits should clearly define their budget development strategies and communicate them to unit and program heads. This concept helps build wide support for budget decisions and avoids time-consuming conflicts and adjustments in the future. Unclear or uncontrolled budget development is likely to create implementation problems. The following subsections present four strategies that can help increase the accuracy and efficiency of budget development:

Strategy 1   Setting annual organizational outcome goals from the top down to guide development of draft program and unit budgets

Strategy 2   Setting annual income and expense targets from the top down to guide development of draft program and unit budgets

Strategy 3   Requesting draft budgets from program and unit heads that show priorities for increased, decreased, and unchanged total budget amounts

Strategy 4   Zero-based budgeting

The first two strategies favor top-down approaches to budget development and thus tend to limit program or unit heads' input. The second two strategies emphasize bottom-up approaches and thus tend to provide program and unit managers with more input. Each strategy has its own strengths and weaknesses, and elements of each can be combined to suit an organization's needs and style. The subsections that follow discuss each of these four strategies and provide worksheets to guide their planning and use.

1. Setting Annual Organizational Outcome Goals from the Top Down

This strategy calls for top management to consult with program and unit managers and appropriate staff before any initial draft budgets are developed.

Defining the overall organization's or specific programs' measurable outcome goals in advance provides a framework for managers and board members to make sure that (1) specific draft budgets and plans for the coming year actively support and further the established outcome goals and (2) that everyone involved has a clear understanding of what needs to be done.

Top management must assess what resources will be available for the next fiscal year based on the most recent income and expense figures and projections, as well as the outcome goals for the coming year. (The outcome goals may apply to the nonprofit as a whole or to individual programs or activities.)

To be effective, the outcome goals must be both specific and measurable. Many nonprofits require quantifiable *performance measures* or *performance indicators* that will demonstrate achievement of specific outcome goals. Quantifiable outcome goals have the added benefit of being useful as a basis for ongoing performance reporting. Following are examples of outcome goals and performance measures:

- **Sample Outcome Goals**
  1. Increase the number of weatherized owner-occupied housing units from 350 to 475 over a twelve-month period
  2. Reduce the average per-unit monthly heating cost by 5 percent

- **Sample Performance Measures**
  1. The actual number of housing units weatherized
  2. Actual reductions in monthly heating costs based on a comparison of heating bills for the same month of the year before and after services were provided

- **Sample Outcome Goals**
  1. Develop and implement a model employment skills training program by June 1 of the next fiscal year
  2. Provide training in the next twelve months to 250 low-income unemployed persons to improve their chances of job placement
  3. Place at least 65 percent of the target population in full-time jobs within two months of completing training

- **Sample Performance Measures**
  1. Implementation of the program by the specified date
  2. Number of clients enrolled in and completing training
  3. Number of clients employed two months after training

With this strategy, the specified outcome goals become the basis for program or unit managers to develop their draft budgets. Outcome goals and performance measures also contribute to the coming year's overall operating plan, providing a clear statement of what the overall organization intends to achieve and how results will be measured.

Use the worksheet in Exhibit 5.1 to plan when and how to carry out this top-down strategy.

These are some follow-through actions required of those managing the budgeting process:

- Include the year's board-approved goals in the package for developing draft budgets to be distributed to applicable unit heads.

- Unit heads must make sure their units' draft budgets include a brief narrative explaining how continuing activities, new initiatives, or proposed changes in their draft budgets will contribute to the nonprofit's overall goals for the coming year.

- In deciding on the final budget, top management and board members should use the narrative explanations in each draft budget to help assess the potential merits and contributions of each to the nonprofit's goals for the coming year.

2. Setting Annual Income and Expense Targets from the Top Down

Under this top-down budget development strategy, top management first sets expense and income targets for the coming year for the organization as a whole and each individual unit. In this way, units know in advance the income that is available (and the

EXHIBIT 5.1   Worksheet for Setting Annual Top-Down Organizational Outcome Goals to Guide Development of Draft Program and Unit Budgets

1. List top management's initial ideas for the coming year's outcome goals to recommend to the board.
   (Consult the organization's written mission statement in developing them.)

2. List when and how top management will present their initial outcome-goal ideas to program and unit managers.

3. List when top management will discuss their outcome goals and get input from unit managers.
   (Gain input before deciding on final recommendations to the board, so as to get additional viewpoints, speed buy-in, and help unite everyone behind final decisions.)

4. After discussion with and input from unit heads, list top management's revised recommendations to the board for the coming year's organizational outcome goals.
   (State desired outcome goals clearly and specifically in order of priority.)

5. List the organization's final, board-approved outcome goals for the coming year.
   (State them clearly and specifically in order of priority.)

income they are expected to generate) during the coming year. Then each unit can develop a draft budget based on the income and expense targets.

Use the checklist in Exhibit 5.2 to plan when and how to carry out this top-down strategy.

EXHIBIT 5.2   **Checklist for Setting Annual Top-Down Income and Expense Targets to Guide Development of Draft Program and Unit Budgets**

___ 1. Top management forms a working group.
(List the members of the working group below, along with target dates for completion.)

___ 2. The working group creates:

a. Reasonably reliable projections (that is, a bare-bones estimate) of unavoidable expenses and desirable or hoped-for expense increases for the organization as a whole

b. A projection of income fairly certain to be received and one of income likely to be received, again for the entire organization.

___ 3. The working group summarizes the fiscal position of the nonprofit as a whole for next year, using the group's expense and income projections as a basis.

___ 4. The working group recommends expense and income targets for all programs, units, and activities, based on estimated resources and expenses.

___ 5. Top management reviews the working group's assumptions, calculations, and targets, making changes as appropriate, and submits them to the board.
(Having the board approve income and expense targets can help avoid potential conflict among managers.)

___ 6. Top management clearly communicates board-approved income and expense targets to managers and unit heads in the package of information on developing draft budgets.

3. Requesting Draft Budgets from Program and Unit Heads That Show Priorities

This strategy calls for each unit head to prepare three draft budgets for the coming year based on a range of percentage variations determined by top management and the board. There are three steps:

Step 1   Top management decides what the percentage of variation should be between the three total draft budgets, for instance, (a) unchanged from this year's total, (b) 3 percent higher, and (c) 3 percent lower. (In any given year, all three draft budgets may reflect differing rates of decreases, or increases, or whatever combination top management and the board call for.)

Step 2   Each unit head prepares the three draft budgets to reflect the unit's priorities and includes a brief summary in each draft budget of the likely impact the specific changes will have on the unit's operations.

Step 3   Top management and the board adjust each unit's draft budget up or down, depending on the most up-to-date understanding of the coming year's income and expenses, and informed by each unit's perspective on change.

The budget team should use the worksheet in Exhibit 5.3 to help plan, introduce, coordinate, and monitor the use of this approach.

EXHIBIT 5.3   **Worksheet for Program and Unit Heads to Prepare Draft Budgets Showing Priorities for Increased, Decreased, and Unchanged Total Budget Amounts**

List the percentage variation from this year's unit budget total that top management decides each program or unit head must include in the three draft budgets for the coming year:

1. A total of _____ percent more than this year's unit budget

2. A total of _____ percent less than this year's unit budget

3. The same total amount as this year's unit budget

4. Implementing Zero-Based Budgeting

Zero-based budgeting (ZBB) focuses on the thorough reevaluation of each of an organization's programs, units, and activities to determine if it should be continued (and, if so, how) and included in the next budget. The ZBB process requires that management justify the existence of every facet of the organization; essentially, ZBB has no built-in assumptions or automatically included items.

a. Elements of Zero-Based Budgeting. Those using ZBB are starting the budgeting process from zero (as opposed to using prior budgetary figures to build on in creating the next budget). Another way to think of ZBB is that the process demands an answer to the question: "If we were not already doing this, knowing what we know now, would we still choose to do it?"

Managers must address more specific questions as well when beginning a ZBB process—for example:

- Should a given program, activity, or position be continued, or would other activities be more important or appropriate?

- If the program, activity, or position is justified, should it continue operating in the same manner, or should it be modified?

- If modified, how will it be modified, when, and by whom?

- How much should the organization spend on the program, activity, or position being studied?

The next step in ZBB is to require every segment of the operating unit to do the following:

- Identify the major functions or activities it performs.

- Answer the preceding four questions as they pertain to the operating unit.

- Create alternatives or options based on the answers to the questions.

- Project anticipated revenues and costs related to each option or alternative.

Exploring and answering these questions can lead management to the following options:

- Abandon the specific unit, program, or activity, perhaps in favor of other, more effective options.

- Change, strengthen, simplify, redirect, reorganize, outsource, or otherwise change the existing effort.

- Make no changes.

b. Possible Problems with Zero-Based Budgeting. ZBB can help nonprofits, particularly very well managed ones, improve their efficiency, effectiveness, and productivity. However, it is not a panacea, nor is it particularly easy. The following are potential difficulties that may arise while attempting ZBB:

- ZBB must have dependable, detailed cost information available from the accounting system (which is not always possible).

- ZBB often feels very threatening to both managers and staff because it involves evaluating, making comparisons, and deciding on desired changes.

- ZBB requires fairly detailed planning and cost calculations and can be made even more difficult and time consuming if it is introduced organizationwide rather than piloted and phased in over time.

- In the real world it is difficult to overlook the prior year's assumptions and data.

Despite these possible problems, ZBB obviously has many benefits, not the least of which is that it encourages managers to look at a broader range of options than they would if using incremental budgeting (Strategies 1 through 3). Nevertheless, because of the potential difficulties, we recommend that organizations experiment with this technique before applying it in a full budgeting process. Using ZBB initially for just one or two programs will allow for a better understanding of its most beneficial application and its strengths and weaknesses.

Use the worksheet in Exhibit 5.4 to plan when and how to carry out this strategy.

D. Budgeting Calendars

The budgeting calendar shows the entire budget development cycle. Setting up a budgeting calendar includes the following steps:

Step 1   Listing the major budget development tasks

Step 2   Establishing the budgeting timetable, including specific deadlines for completing each task

Step 3   Identifying the persons responsible for accomplishing each task

Step 4   Obtaining input from the board and staff

Step 5   Revising and distributing the finalized budgeting calendar

The budget development calendar should be reviewed each year and revised, based on last year's experience and any anticipated changes. The following subsections explain each step in creating a budgeting calendar.

1. Listing Major Budget Development Tasks

Major budget cycle tasks may vary depending on the size of a nonprofit and the overall budget development strategy it adopts. For instance, larger nonprofits may need lengthy data-gathering and planning processes that include multiple phases and tasks, such as:

- Developing guidelines for salary and price increases

- Preparing or updating income and expense estimates

- Reviewing and updating long-range financial and strategic plans

- Establishing income and expense goals for programs and departments

- Developing budget priorities, guidelines, and instructions for the coming year

**EXHIBIT
5.4**   **Worksheet for Zero-Based Budgeting**

1. List by whom, when, and how the ZBB approach will be explained to unit heads and others.

2. Identify the specific training that people in finance and other programs and units will get to understand and implement the ZBB approach.

3. List each of the organization's units, programs, and activities that are to be reviewed and analyzed, along with the level of financial and other resources currently committed to and generated by each.

4. List which individuals in each unit, program, or activity will be sent the appropriate parts of the list for review, analysis, and option building.

5. Describe the various options or models that have emerged from each unit's answering the question: "If we were not already doing this, knowing what we now know, would we do it the same way?"

6. List the anticipated income and costs for each model or option (use varying activity levels when appropriate).

7. Describe whether each specific program, function, or activity should be eliminated, modified, or continued relatively unchanged.

Smaller nonprofits may require somewhat shorter planning processes and fewer phases and tasks. Regardless of the nonprofit's size, however, the CFO's first step is to think through the entire budget development cycle and clearly define what must be done.

2. Establishing Overall Time Frames and Specific Deadlines

Deciding when to begin and end the overall budget development process depends heavily on the size of the nonprofit and the complexity of the specific budget development strategy chosen.

Budgeting processes that involve active participation by program and unit managers should begin at least seven months before the budget must go into effect. Longer lead times give top management more time to prepare needed budgeting guidelines, materials, and instructions, and allow program and unit managers more time to develop draft budgets.

At the same time, however, long lead times also mean fewer months or quarters of current-year financial information are available to help project actual income and expenses into the coming year. Thus the need for accurate projections based on current financial data must be weighed against the need for a realistic time allotment for completing important budgeting steps.

3. Identifying Those Responsible for Each Task

Establish accountability for completing each budgeting task by identifying the individual responsible for ensuring completion of each required task by the deadline. This way, everyone knows who is supposed to do what in developing the budget.

4. Obtaining Input from the Board and Staff

Obtaining feedback from the board and staff on the draft budget cycle and calendar provides two benefits. First, members of the board and staff may identify aspects of the draft budget cycle and calendar that others may have overlooked in compiling these documents. Second, board and staff members may be able to recognize when deadlines are unrealistic from their individual or departmental perspective. Review by support and clerical staff can also be helpful, as they may be able to provide useful input and an accurate estimate of the time required to prepare and duplicate budget development instructions and materials.

5. Revising and Distributing the Finalized Budgeting Calendar

In revising and distributing the finalized budget calendar to the board and staff, it is critical that everyone involved in or affected by the budgeting process be clearly informed of the steps in the process, the budgeting schedule, and what is expected of them. Whenever the budgeting calendar is modified, the changes should be communicated in writing to the same people who received the first draft calendar.

A sample budgeting calendar for a large nonprofit is shown in Exhibit 5.5.

EXHIBIT 5.5   **Sample Budgeting Calendar for a Large Nonprofit**

DEADLINE DATE	MAJOR TASKS	RESPONSIBLE PERSON(S)
6/1	Meet to review strategic plans, goals, and objectives.	Board, CEO, and CFO
6/15	Prepare income and expense forecasts and set budget targets, budgeting policies, and procedures; prepare budgeting materials, guidelines, and instructions.	CEO and CFO
7/1	Plan and hold kickoff meeting; present major budget development policies and guidelines, materials, and instructions to unit and program managers.	CFO
8/1	Follow up by giving unit and program managers any needed budget development training and additional materials needed, and by identifying specific Finance Department staff to contact for help.	CFO and finance staff
9/1	Unit and program managers prepare draft budgets and backup documentation by deadline, following policies and instructions.	Unit and program managers
10/1	Consolidate all draft budgets and income and expense projections into one; submit to top management by deadline.	CFO
10/15	Top management reviews draft budgets and discusses them with unit and program managers to arrive at any revisions.	CEO and CFO
11/1	Prepare final, revised overall and unit and program budget documents for presentation to the board.	CFO
11/15	Present budget to board for its review, discussion, modification, and approval.	CEO and CFO
11/30	Incorporate all board-approved changes into final budget documents.	CFO and finance staff
12/15	Distribute approved budget to top management, unit, and program heads, and any other appropriate people.	CFO

Note

Ideally, an organization's budgeting cycle will correspond to the natural cycle of its business. This means that in determining the beginning and ending points of their budget cycles, organizations must take into account such factors as their fiscal year start date and the reporting requirements of funding sources and regulatory entities.

E. Budgeting Goals, Guidelines, Policies, and Procedures

Establishing budgeting goals, guidelines, policies, and procedures is essential to creating the overall context of budgeting for the coming year. To start this process, the board, CEO, and CFO should review the nonprofit's mission, current fiscal status, and projected income and expenses for the coming year. Nonprofits with long-range financial plans usually also update them at this time, using current information to project fiscal and program trends likely to affect operations.

Based on their review and the specific budget development strategy they have chosen, the board, CEO, and CFO then set organizationwide operating budget goals for income and expenses for the coming year. The goals they set will be used to help guide development of the coming year's organizationwide operating budget, as well as individual program and unit operating budgets.

1. Setting Guidelines for Developing Operating Budgets

Often the board of directors, CEO, and CFO all have input in establishing policies and guidelines for developing the coming year's budget, including matters related to:

- Specific program objectives and priorities

- Income and expense targets or limits

- Policies governing the creation of new programs or positions

- Guidelines for existing personnel costs, such as wage increases and fringe-benefit rates

2. Identifying Priorities in the Development of Operating Budgets

Effectively identifying priorities is contingent on a thorough understanding of an up-to-date and clearly defined mission statement. An accurate mission statement is necessary to guide programs—especially during planning and budgeting activities—because it summarizes an organization's basic purposes and primary reason for existence. A good mission statement can help your organization do several important things:

- Set clear organizational and program goals

- Make sure current and proposed programs and activities are appropriate

- Focus resources productively

- Help determine the specific activities and expenditures that should be maintained and the ones that should be reduced or eliminated

Reviewing the mission statement should be the first step in determining organizational or program priorities. The next step might include an examination of:

- Demographics of your service area

- Specific realistic needs of your clients

- Actual response to your existing programs

Assessing existing programs (or any service gap or problem that becomes evident) using the criteria already described will provide important information to help identify priorities. For example, if it becomes clear that a certain program seems to meet community needs perfectly yet has an unexpectedly low rate of usage and little community support, a budget priority might be to conduct further research to determine the cause of this situation.

3. Setting Organizationwide Operating-Budget Goals

The board, CEO, and CFO work together to set total organizationwide operating income and expense goals. They determine:

- The total amount of income the organization as a whole expects to take in during the coming year

- The total amount the organization as a whole expects to spend to carry out all its activities during the coming year

Total operating income and total operating expenses should generally match. If organizationwide expense goals exceed income goals, meaning that anticipated expenses will exceed anticipated income, then the board, CEO, and CFO should:

- Refigure total operating income and expense projections

- Be prepared to take corrective action later, such as cutting budgeted costs or generating additional income

- Formally decide to use funds from the organization's unrestricted funds to make up the difference

- Take the risk of operating at a deficit during the coming year (which is not recommended and is certainly not a sustainable strategy)

If organizationwide income projections exceed expense projections, meaning that estimated income is more than estimated expenses, then the board, CEO, and CFO should:

- Adjust the total operating income and expense projections so they match

- Let the surplus stand, as a hedge against unexpected costs during the coming year

- Designate the surplus for future use as needed

4. Setting Individual Program and Unit Operating-Budget Goals

The CFO and CEO should work with managers of each individual program and unit to set program and unit income and expense projections for the coming year, based on the organizationwide income and expense projections. In turn, each program and unit manager should use individual program or unit income and expense projections to guide planning for the nature, staffing, and outcome goals of the specific program or unit (and for the line item detail in the program or unit operating budget). Total anticipated operating income and expenses for each individual program or unit should match. If they do not match, plans for alternative income generation must be developed, or expenses must be cut. Developing the discipline and knowledge to perform these steps can make a big difference in the future health of your organization.

Projecting income and expenses is easier, and the results more accurate and understandable, if written policies and procedures exist to provide program and unit managers with necessary guidance. The following are recommendations for establishing effective budgeting policies and procedures:

- **Suggestions for Establishing Basic Budgeting Policies and Procedures**
  1. Identify the specific steps, responsibilities, and timetables in the budgeting cycle and the budgeting calendar.
  2. Identify those responsible for preparing and disseminating the budgeting package to be used in preparing budget estimates.
  3. Identify the contents and format of the overall budgeting package to be used in preparing draft budgets and the format to be used in preparing draft budgets themselves.
  4. Identify the number of actual draft budgets to be prepared by program and unit managers. Options include a draft budget showing estimated increases in income or expenses, one showing no change, one showing estimated decreases in income or expenses, or any combination of these.
  5. Identify those responsible for preparing draft budgets and approving them.
  6. Identify processes for modifying in-house and funding-source budgets.

- **Suggestions for Establishing Basic Income Projection Policies and Procedures**
  1. Identify those responsible for estimating and approving proposed changes in income.
  2. Identify the percentage of change to existing income for program and unit managers to use in preparing draft budgets. Options include a percentage increase, no change, a percentage decrease, or any combination of these. Be sure to communicate in advance with all current and potential funding sources regarding any possible changes in funding or eligibility for specific funds.
  3. Identify those responsible for estimating and approving the certainty of receiving anticipated income from individual funding sources.
  4. Identify the level of certainty needed to include anticipated funds in the category of projected income in preparing draft program and unit budgets.

- **Suggestions for Establishing Basic Expense Projection Policies and Procedures**
  1. Identify those responsible for estimating and approving proposed changes in expenses.

2. Identify the percentage of change to existing salaries, wages, and fringe benefits to be used in preparing draft budgets. Options include a percentage increase, no change, a percentage decrease, or any combination of these.

3. Identify the methods for making changes to existing expenses in preparing draft budgets. Options include estimating a percentage increase or decrease, determining actual increases or decreases (by checking leases and catalogues and negotiating with suppliers and vendors), or both.

4. Identify the methods for determining the amount of any new expenses for the coming budget year. Options include determining actual amounts (by checking leases, union contracts, and supply catalogues and contacting and negotiating with suppliers and vendors).

CHAPTER 6

6 Cash Flow Forecasting

As noted throughout this book, effective operational budgeting must be in place in order to create effective, useful, and reliable cash flow forecasts. *The Budget-Building Book for Nonprofits* (by Murray Dropkin and Bill La Touche; Jossey-Bass, 1998) provides comprehensive and practical guidance, information, and tools for developing sound budgeting processes. In Chapter Five we summarized the relevant parts of *The Budget-Building Book for Nonprofits* as an overview of the operational budget development process. We included this overview to stress the point that having effective operational budgeting processes in place is essential to building accurate cash flow forecasts. This chapter offers instructions and examples on how operating budgets may be used to develop specific types of cash flow forecasts. (Readers who are not familiar with organizational budgeting should see Chapter Five or, for a more comprehensive treatment of the topic, *The Budget-Building Book for Nonprofits*.)

A. Fundamentals of Cash Flow Forecasting

One of the fundamental differences between developing cash flow forecasts and operating budgets is in the accounting basis that is used for each. "Accrual-basis" accounting, which recognizes all income as it is earned (whether received or not) and all expenses as they are incurred (whether paid or not), should be used in operating-budget development. Cash flow forecasts, however, will be constructed using "cash-basis" accounting, which includes only the money that is physically received and paid out. Therefore, the first step in using the organization's operating budget to develop cash flow forecasts is to eliminate the effect of accruals. This step will require two main actions:

1. Cash-Basis Accounting for Cash Inflows

For cash-basis purposes only money that will be received and deposited by the organization in the budget period should be recognized as cash inflow. For example, assume an organization holds a fundraising event for which 80 percent of the event's total expected proceeds is paid at the door as admission fees and 20 percent consists of promises to make contributions that will not be received until the next fiscal period.

The accounting profession differentiates between the terms *forecast* and *projection*. For the purposes of this book, however, we have used the two terms interchangeably.

The cash flow forecast for the period during which the event is held should only include the cash that will actually be received during that period. Contributions that were promised and will be received during a future fiscal period will be included in the cash flow forecast for the period during which they are actually received.

Calculating the cash inflow side of a cash flow forecast presents the challenge of recognizing as cash inflow only items that will be collected during the reporting period. To make the forecast as accurate as possible, the organization should examine cash collection rates for prior events. Organizations may also compare their accounts receivable balance with prior-year balances. Prior collection patterns and current characteristics will help in estimating the likely percentage of collection. These two components—immediately realizable cash and collection of receivables—will normally represent most of the cash inflow that should be recognized in the cash flow forecast. Obviously, there will be situations in which organizations will have other sources of cash inflow that should be included in forecasts. For example, in developing cash flow forecasts for Universal Nonprofit, proceeds from a bank loan had to be recognized as cash inflow in the cash flow forecast covering the fiscal period during which the loan was received.

2. Cash-Basis Accounting for Cash Outflows

The outflow component of the cash flow forecast will only include cash paid out by the organization for expenses and any cash payments made to pay down accounts payable or other liabilities. Depreciation and amortization expenses will not be included in forecasted cash outflows because they do not represent actual payments of cash.

A brief example will help illustrate some differences between cash-basis accounting and accrual-basis accounting. Suppose that an organization has an accrual-basis operating budget with expenses totaling $575,000. This figure includes a calculation of amortization- and depreciation-related expenses of $45,000. During the budget period, the organization will pay down $25,000 of debt. Accounts payable will increase by $15,000. These data would be treated in a cash flow forecast as follows:

- The $25,000 used to pay down a loan is a cash outflow that would not be included in an operating budget but that *would* be included in a cash flow forecast. Paying down a previously incurred liability is not an expense; it is simply a reduction in a liability. However, because money is actually paid out, this amount must be shown as an outflow on the cash flow forecast.

- The $45,000 allocated to amortization and depreciation is not a cash transaction and therefore would not be included in the cash flow forecast as an outflow. Amortization and depreciation are noncash expenses that spread the cost of acquiring an asset over a certain period of time. Money paid to acquire an asset in a prior fiscal period has no impact on the current period's cash flow. The current period has amortization and depreciation expenses, but the cash outflow occurred in a prior period.

- The $15,000 increase in accounts payable indicates that the organization financed $15,000 of its operations by incurring additional accounts payable. But because this amount was not actually paid during the forecast period, it should not be included as a cash outflow in the cash flow forecast.

Exhibit 6.1 shows how the expenses shown in the accrual-basis operating budget would be converted to the appropriate cash-basis expense figure to use in a cash flow forecast.

The aforementioned analysis only identifies the total outflow of cash. Next we must identify timing issues relating to cash flow. As is evident from the example just given, cash flow forecasts are summaries of the actual cash transactions for a given fiscal period. Money deposited and money paid out are the only transactions that will be included in cash flow forecasts. Keeping this concept in mind will make converting information from accrual-basis operating budgets into information applicable to cash-basis cash flow forecasting a relatively simple task for smaller organizations.

B. Cash Flow Forecasting Based on the Operating Budget

The process of creating cash flow budgets from the operating budget will involve reviewing and characterizing each line item in the operating budget. Identifying, analyzing, and determining how each line item of the operating budget affects cash flow and the month affected will provide additional necessary information for cash flow forecast development. The steps in this process are described in the following subsections.

1. Reviewing the Operating Budget

The first step in developing an accurate cash flow forecast is to review the organizational operating budget and assess the cash flow effect of each line item. To do this for your organization, you must figure out how each income or expense item will affect cash inflow or outflow. For example, rent expense must normally be paid on time, or

EXHIBIT 6.1	Summary of Conversion from Operating Budget to Cash Flow Forecast

Total Expenses per Operating Budget (Accrual Basis)	$575,000
Add Repayment of Debt (Cash Outflow)	25,000
	$600,000
Subtract Increase in Accounts Payable (No Cash Outflow)	(15,000)
Subtract Depreciation and Amortization (No Cash Outflow)	(45,000)
Total Cash Outflows Identified for Cash Flow Forecast	$540,000

the organization will face legal action. Thus rent expense will be a fairly straightforward cash outflow. Some operating-budget items may be paid over a longer period of time by negotiating with vendors. Organizations that choose to finance such items will have to consider the effect of doing so in the cash outflow component of their cash flow forecasts. Decisions regarding renting versus purchasing equipment and buying real property outright versus obtaining a mortgage will have impacts on cash flow. Conversely, budgeted noncash items like depreciation and amortization have no effect on the cash flow forecast and will be eliminated in the conversion of items from the operating budget for use in the cash flow forecast.

After each line item in the operating budget has been analyzed and the cash flow effect and timing have been determined, the organization may begin to prepare the cash flow forecast.

2. Adjusting the Operating Budget to Create the Cash Flow Forecast

The second step in this process is modifying the information in the operating budget so that it can be incorporated into the cash flow forecast. The best way to approach this is to set up a worksheet like the one shown in Exhibit 6.2. The leftmost column will contain the operating-budget line items. The next column will contain the expense amounts from the operating budget. The third column will show any cash-related adjustments to the operating-budget amounts. The fourth column will indicate the cash flow effect of the operating-budget line item.

When there is a direct relationship between the operating-budget item and the cash flow forecast item, there will be no adjustment necessary to incorporate the amount into the cash flow forecast. Line items that have a cash flow effect may require adjustments to operating-budget amounts in order to include them with accuracy in cash flow forecasts. For example, if your organization is acquiring new furniture at a cost of $50,000 and you are leasing it over five years, cash flow will be affected for the five-year period (as opposed to paying for the furniture in one payment, which would only affect cash flow for the period in which the payment was made).

Prior experience and future expectations will determine the adjustments your organization will have to make to include operating-budget amounts in cash flow forecasts. Items such as rent, utilities, and salaries should all have a direct effect on cash flow and will usually not require an adjustment. Supplies, maintenance, and equipment purchases and similar line items may vary in their effect on cash flow, based on financing plans. Items such as depreciation and amortization will have to be flagged for elimination from the cash flow forecast.

3. Reviewing and Approving the Cash Flow Forecast

The annual cash flow forecast should be reviewed, and the beginning cash balance should be added to the net cash flow (cash inflow less cash outflow) to determine what the forecasted year-ending cash balance will be. Adjustments may have to be made to the planned cash payments for the year if the cash balances are too low.

EXHIBIT 6.2 **Sample Worksheet for Preparing an Annual Cash Flow Forecast**

Universal Nonprofit
Annual Cash Flow Forecast Worksheet
Fiscal Year 2000

BUDGET CATEGORY	ACCRUAL BUDGET	ADJUSTMENTS	EXPLANATION	CASH OUTFLOW
Personnel	$1,153,163	$(53,163)[a]	Accrued compensation	$1,100,000
Consultants and Professional Services	107,022	(82,022)[b]	Deferred payment arrangement	25,000
Materials and Supplies	114,613	—	N/A	114,613
Facility Costs	119,014	—	N/A	119,014
Specific Assistance to Clients	89,873	—	N/A	89,873
Other Costs	74,977	—	N/A	74,977
Total Operating Costs	$1,658,662	—	N/A	$1,523,477
Capital Equipment	60,000	(46,000)[c]	Equipment financed	14,000
Totals	$1,718,662	$(181,185)		$1,537,477

[a]Adjustment to illustrate *payment* in fiscal year 2001 of personnel expenses *incurred* in fiscal year 2000.
[b]Adjustment to illustrate *payment* in fiscal year 2001 of consultant expenses *incurred* in fiscal year 2000.
[c]Adjustment to show acquisition of equipment via a deposit of $14,000 in fiscal year 2000 with balance of $46,000 due in a future period.

C. Short-Term Cash Flow Forecasting

Short-term cash flow forecasts should be designed to meet your organization's needs. Annual cash flow forecasts may be broken into whatever time periods will be most useful. Different sizes and types of organizations will benefit from different frequencies of cash flow forecasting. For example, in the case of a foundation with most of its assets in investments, cash flow forecasts on an annual basis may be all that is necessary. If your organization receives diverse types of funding, such as funding from many special events or contribution sources, your cash forecasting will be much more complicated and challenging and should be done more frequently. Organizations that prepare daily, weekly, quarterly, or annual cash flow forecasts should see Exhibits 6.3, 6.4, 6.5, and 6.6, respectively, for examples.

In cash flow forecasts the cash inflow and cash outflow items should be put into the time period they are expected to be received or paid out. For example, periodic items such as rent are distributed throughout the year. Personnel expenses may fluctuate if there is seasonal demand for the services the organization provides. In addition, cash flow forecasts should show both the beginning and ending cash balances. Each of these

EXHIBIT 6.3 Sample Daily Cash Flow Forecast

ABC Nonprofit
Daily Cash Flow Forecast
Week Ending: _____

	Monday	Tuesday	Wednesday	Thursday	Friday	Total
Opening Cash Balance	$270,649	$262,612	$256,590	$246,038	$239,260	$270,649
Cash Inflows:						
Revenue 1	$7,186	$4,312	$10,780	$5,390	$8,264	$35,932
Revenue 2	3,054	1,832	4,581	2,290	3,512	15,269
Revenue 3	2,335	1,401	3,503	1,751	2,686	11,676
Revenue 4	1,796	1,078	2,695	1,347	2,066	8,982
Revenue 5	1,437	862	2,156	1,078	1,652	7,185
Revenue 6	1,257	754	1,886	943	1,446	6,286
Revenue 7	898	539	1,347	673	1,033	4,490
Total Cash Inflow	$17,963	$10,778	$26,948	$13,472	$ 20,659	$89,820
Total Cash Available	$288,612	$273,390	$283,538	$259,510	$259,919	$360,469
Cash Outflows:						
Payroll	$—	$—	$—	$—	$—	$—
Payroll Taxes	—	—	—	—	—	—
Health Insurance	—	—	—	—	—	—
Consultants	9,000	5,400	13,500	6,750	10,350	45,000
Rent	—	—	—	—	—	—
Other Costs	14,000	8,400	21,000	10,500	16,100	70,000
Capital Purchases	—	—	—	—	—	—
Loan Repayments	3,000	3,000	3,000	3,000	3,000	15,000
Total Cash Outflow	$26,000	$16,800	$37,500	$20,250	$29,450	$130,000
Closing Cash Balance	$262,612	$256,590	$246,038	$239,260	$230,469	$230,469

Note: A few nonprofit organizations do a daily cash flow forecast. A schedule of cash balances by bank account with only a total column shown for weekends is far more common.

EXHIBIT 6.4 Sample Weekly Cash Flow Forecast

ABC Nonprofit
Weekly Cash Flow Forecast
for Thirteen Weeks Ending: _____

	Week 1	Week 2	Week 3	Week 4	Week 5	Week 6	Week 7	Week 8	Week 9	Week 10	Week 11	Week 12	Week 13	Total
Opening Cash Balance	$270,649	$230,469	$66,969	$47,080	$(121,256)	$130,574	$(17,926)	$256,074	$44,404	$222,345	$32,175	$77,839	$28,669	$270,649
Cash Inflows:														
Revenue 1	35,932	34,600	29,600	54,267	152,733	40,600	161,600	52,933	108,733	41,933	54,267	101,933	72,427	941,558
Revenue 2	15,269	14,705	12,580	23,063	64,911	17,255	68,680	22,496	46,211	17,821	23,063	43,321	30,781	400,156
Revenue 3	11,676	11,245	9,620	17,636	49,638	15,195	52,520	17,203	35,338	13,628	17,636	33,128	23,538	306,001
Revenue 4	8,982	8,650	7,400	13,566	38,183	10,150	40,400	13,233	27,183	10,483	13,566	25,483	18,106	235,385
Revenue 5	7,185	6,920	5,920	10,853	30,546	8,120	32,320	10,586	21,746	8,386	10,853	20,386	14,485	188,306
Revenue 6	6,286	6,055	5,180	9,496	26,728	7,105	28,280	9,263	19,028	7,338	9,496	17,838	12,674	164,767
Revenue 7	4,490	4,325	3,700	6,783	19,091	5,075	20,200	6,616	13,591	5,241	6,783	12,741	9,053	117,689
Total Cash Inflow	$89,820	$86,500	$74,000	$135,664	$381,830	$101,500	$404,000	$132,330	$271,830	$104,830	$135,664	$254,830	$181,064	$2,353,862
Total Cash Available	$360,469	$316,969	$140,969	$182,744	$260,574	$232,074	$386,074	$388,404	$316,234	$327,175	$167,839	$332,669	$209,733	$2,624,511
Cash Outflows:														
Payroll	$—	$170,100	$—	$170,100	$—	$170,100	$—	$200,340	$—	$204,120	$—	$170,100	$90,405	$1,175,265
Payroll Taxes	—	21,150	—	21,150	—	21,150	—	24,910	—	25,380	—	21,150	11,240	146,130
Health Insurance	—	—	—	34,000	—	—	—	34,000	—	—	—	34,000	8,500	110,500
Employee Benefits	—	33,750	—	33,750	—	33,750	—	39,750	—	40,500	—	33,750	17,937	233,187
Consultants	45,000	—	35,000	—	35,000	—	35,000	—	35,000	—	35,000	—	18,333	238,333
Rent	—	—	—	20,000	—	—	—	20,000	—	—	—	20,000	5,000	65,000
Other Costs	70,000	25,000	40,000	25,000	80,000	25,000	80,000	25,000	40,000	25,000	40,000	25,000	41,666	541,666
Capital Purchases	—	—	—	—	—	—	—	—	—	—	—	—	—	
Loan Repayments	15,000	—	18,889	—	15,000	—	15,000	—	18,889	—	15,000	—	8,148	105,926
Total Cash Outflow	$130,000	$250,000	$93,889	$304,000	$130,000	$250,000	$130,000	$344,000	$93,889	$295,000	$90,000	$304,000	$201,229	$2,616,007
Closing Cash Balance	$230,469	$66,969	$47,080	$(121,256)	$130,574	$(17,926)	$256,074	$44,404	$222,345	$32,175	$77,839	$28,669	$8,504	$8,504

Note: For organizations in tight cash flow circumstances with little working capital, this is a desirable report as it provides vital information. For example, this report indicates that at the end of week 4, a $(121,256) cash deficit is occurring, as well as another deficit of $(17,926) in week 6. In addition, some low balances appear at the end of weeks 10, 12, and 13. This organization should plan on getting a line of credit of at least $200,000 to guard against possible cash deficits or unexpected occurrences requiring cash.

EXHIBIT 6.5   **Sample Quarterly Cash Flow Forecast**

ABC Nonprofit
Quarterly Cash Flow Forecast
Fiscal Year 2000

	FIRST QUARTER	SECOND QUARTER	THIRD QUARTER	FOURTH QUARTER	TOTAL
OPENING CASH BALANCE	$270,649	$8,504	$(114,984)	$(135,469)	$270,649
CASH INFLOWS:					
Revenue 1	$941,558	$912,592	$962,785	$1,001,296	$3,818,231
Revenue 2	400,156	361,994	358,374	379,876	1,500,400
Revenue 3	306,001	285,293	290,999	285,645	1,167,938
Revenue 4	235,385	215,111	225,866	232,642	909,004
Revenue 5	188,306	179,041	188,889	185,111	741,347
Revenue 6	164,767	148,295	154,968	160,392	628,422
Revenue 7	117,689	111,358	114,698	118,139	461,884
Total Cash Inflow	$2,353,862	$2,213,684	$2,296,579	$2,363,101	$9,227,226
Total Cash Available	$2,624,511	$2,222,188	$2,181,595	$2,227,632	$9,497,875
CASH OUTFLOWS:					
Payroll	$1,175,265	$1,067,750	$1,080,655	$1,060,765	$4,384,435
Payroll Taxes	146,130	127,630	130,567	121,637	525,964
Health Insurance	110,500	97,650	100,475	93,767	402,392
Employee Benefits	233,187	206,975	210,625	197,650	848,437
Consultants	238,333	175,000	165,000	135,750	714,083
Rent	65,000	60,000	62,500	62,500	250,000
Other Costs	541,666	487,500	467,575	425,750	1,922,491
Capital Purchases	—	15,000	—	25,000	40,000
Loan Repayments	105,926	99,667	99,667	101,567	406,827
Total Cash Outflow	$2,616,007	$2,337,172	$2,317,064	$2,224,386	$9,494,629
CLOSING CASH BALANCE	$8,504	$(114,984)	$(135,469)	$3,246	$3,246

components of the forecast is essential to managing cash flow. They will help the organization monitor the cash balance and assist management in identifying excessive balances or potential overdrafts.

Cash balances may vary widely during different fiscal periods as a result of seasonal volume fluctuations, weather, contribution patterns, and other factors. This is why preparing cash flow reports on a frequent basis is very helpful to ongoing cash flow management. As stated previously, however, your organization will need to assess its unique cash flow management needs to determine the frequency and detail of cash flow reporting that will be most beneficial. There is no rule of thumb in this regard.

EXHIBIT 6.6 Sample Annual Cash Flow Forecast

ABC Nonprofit
Annual Cash Flow Forecast
Year Ending December 31

	2000	2001	2002	2003	2004	TOTAL
OPENING CASH BALANCE	$270,649	$3,246	$(193,080)	$84,967	$264,779	$270,649
CASH INFLOWS:						
Revenue 1	$3,818,231	$3,727,081	$3,675,425	$3,550,750	$3,675,985	$18,447,472
Revenue 2	1,500,400	1,440,238	1,410,155	1,375,500	1,260,555	6,986,848
Revenue 3	1,167,938	1,149,503	1,172,493	1,160,575	1,100,660	5,751,169
Revenue 4	909,004	881,995	865,665	825,785	795,235	4,277,684
Revenue 5	741,347	748,676	715,675	685,985	650,785	3,542,468
Revenue 6	628,422	600,364	580,685	550,685	535,155	2,895,311
Revenue 7	461,884	464,159	460,557	455,758	430,125	2,272,483
Total Cash Inflow	$9,227,226	$9,012,016	$8,880,655	$8,605,038	$8,448,500	$44,173,435
Total Cash Available	$9,497,875	$9,015,262	$8,687,575	$8,690,005	$8,713,279	$44,444,084
CASH OUTFLOWS:						
Payroll	$4,384,435	$4,186,679	$4,061,078	$4,020,468	$4,030,499	$20,683,159
Payroll Taxes	525,964	397,734	385,802	381,944	382,897	2,074,341
Health Insurance	402,392	382,075	370,612	359,494	348,709	1,863,282
Employee Benefits	848,437	797,280	765,388	734,773	705,382	3,851,260
Consultants	714,083	647,047	601,754	559,631	520,457	3,042,972
Rent	250,000	226,625	209,628	193,906	179,363	1,059,522
Other Costs	1,922,491	2,150,322	1,825,675	1,749,335	1,723,095	9,370,918
Capital Purchases	40,000	45,000	36,996	150,000	100,000	371,996
Loan Repayments	406,827	375,580	345,675	275,675	225,675	1,629,432
Total Cash Outflow	$9,494,629	$9,208,342	$8,602,608	$8,425,226	$8,216,077	$43,946,882
CLOSING CASH BALANCE	$3,246	$(193,080)	$84,967	$264,779	$497,202	$497,202

Note: This forecast needs careful analysis. It is unsatisfactory to show a $3,246 cash surplus on forecasted inflows of over nine million dollars in fiscal year 2000. Because these are forecasts that are subject to error, the projected surplus of $3,245 is too small. Note the projected $(193,080) cash deficit at the end of fiscal year 2001. This forecast needs to be reworked. Either collections are coming in too slow, or cash is going out too fast. This indicates a cash flow problem.

Our recommendation is that most organizations should, at minimum, prepare quarterly cash flow forecasts, such as the one shown in Exhibit 6.5. (Exhibit A.1 in Resource A is also an example of a report many organizations will find useful.)

The final step in cash flow forecast development is thorough review of the forecasts by both financial managers and operations managers. The timing and amounts of the cash flows should be examined and critiqued. If the draft cash flow forecasts pass this review, the documents may be finalized and any corrective action plans may be implemented.

D. Periodic Review of the Cash Flow Forecast

In addition to review of the draft cash flow forecast by financial and operations managers, proper cash flow forecasting will require organizations to perform regular periodic reviews of finalized forecasts. Actual cash flow will almost never be exactly as anticipated, and the differences between the reality and the projections must be assessed, evaluated, and incorporated into long-term forecasts. An analysis of the sources and uses of cash should be conducted on a regular basis to identify variances. This analysis should include an examination of changes in working capital (current assets less current liabilities), asset acquisitions and other capital expenditures, and the effects of any financing on cash flow forecasts. These processes will provide your organization with a clear picture of the true current cash flow status. It might also help organizations assess how accurate their projection methodologies are and will reveal the precise nature of potential future cash flow problems.

Periodic reviews should also involve recasting shorter-term cash flow forecasts to determine whether or not the annual forecast remains accurate and reliable. Those reviewing cash flow forecasts must assess if variances will impact future cash projections. If it becomes apparent that future cash projections are no longer valid, the organization must take action to secure new sources of cash or cut projects that draw on the organization's cash. Management can take specific actions, such as delaying an equipment purchase, making a request to current donors for additional funds, or restructuring operations. (Chapter Eight details other specific actions that may be taken when cash shortfalls are forecasted.)

Cash flow forecast preparation may present an excellent opportunity for organizations to improve cash flow management. Cash flow forecasts reflecting monthly or weekly cash outflow and inflow can give important insights into the operating plan of the organization and how that plan is affecting cash flow. However, the most important insight that a cash flow forecast provides is the level of cash available at any given time during the forecast period.

E. Corrective Actions for Forecasted Cash Shortages

The organization can pursue several corrective actions when a cash shortage is forecasted. However, the first action that should be taken is to identify what caused the projected cash deficit. Perhaps an equipment purchase was unwisely planned during a period of low cash inflow. When cash balances are low, nonessential purchases should be delayed to conserve cash. However, if greater operating expenses or falling support causes the projected cash shortage, the problem is more serious. The organization must identify the direct cause of the deficiency when forecasted cash shortages are due to operational problems. The organization must also investigate and analyze *cost drivers* (objects or actions that drive costs above an expected amount) so that corrective action may be taken. Such analyses include reviewing materials and processes to determine whether any savings can be attained by using different materials or changing policies and procedures. A line of credit or an interim loan would be an acceptable solution for a short-term cash flow shortage. However, without a corrective plan of action, the problem will return at a later date. The organization may also want to go to significant donors to ask for cash ahead of a normally scheduled date to ease the impact of a cash flow problem. The organization must attempt to obtain advances and increase cash balances through any reasonable means while implementing adjustments to eliminate future cash flow problems. (Strategies for addressing both short-term cash flow problems and more serious cash flow problems can be found in Chapter Eight.)

CHAPTER 7

Cash Flow Reporting, Monitoring, and Analysis

The key to maintaining your organization's financial health is having the capacity to respond to changes in the environment. The nonprofit operating environment is dynamic, owing to both internal and external factors. Organizations must be able to recognize when it will be necessary to modify financial plans, budgets, and cash flow forecasts in response to the environment and to circumstances within the organization. Having formal mechanisms in place for such monitoring and modification will allow your organization to adapt to changes quickly and efficiently.

The most important aspect of monitoring an organization's financial health is being able to identify problems early in a financial cycle. The earlier your organization can identify areas of operations that will require attention or intervention, the more likely it is to correct problems before they cause substantial financial consequences. In order to do this effectively, data collection, analysis, and reporting must be maintained at a high level of accuracy and consistency. Those responsible for monitoring cash flow must receive the required information in a timely, clear, and complete manner. This chapter focuses on the report-monitoring aspect of cash flow management and includes information on how management can use reports to recognize and isolate potential threats to financial health.

Effective cash flow management requires vigilance and flexibility: vigilance in being ever mindful of current and developing situations that might require corrective action and flexibility in being able to modify plans accordingly. Unfortunately, some finance professionals believe it is an admission of failure to redo a budget or cash flow forecast at the halfway point in a fiscal year. In reality, there is nothing farther from the truth. Revising budgets and cash flow forecasts in response to changing circumstances is essential to effective overall financial and cash flow management. Cash is not a theoretical concept. If your organization does not have cash available, it will go out of business. Universal Nonprofit, for example, ended up missing a payroll because of its cash flow problems, which seriously harmed staff morale and confidence. If your organization does not effectively manage cash and fails to pay rent, causing your landlord to start eviction proceedings, it will be hard to run your day-care or counseling center. If your office equipment supplier shows up at your headquarters in the middle of the workday to repossess your copier, your organization will be severely inconvenienced (we have actually seen this happen). Forecasting cash flow must receive serious attention from top management.

In Chapter Six we provided information and instructions on creating cash flow forecasts based on operating budgets. However, these forecasts will only be valuable to the extent that they are used. The following sections discuss some ways these tools may be used as part of an effective report-monitoring package.

A. Cash Receipts and Disbursements Reports

We believe one of the most effective reports for monitoring cash flow forecasts is based on the cash receipts and cash disbursements model. This is a simple model in which input depends on history and reasonable expectations about the future. See Exhibit 7.1 for an example of this type of report.

The first step in creating a cash receipts and disbursements report is to list all your sources of cash by category. The categories you use may be very specific or very broad, depending on your organization's needs and preferences. Common categories include

EXHIBIT 7.1   **Sample Cash Receipts and Disbursements Report**

ABC Organization
Cash Receipts and Disbursements Report
January 1, 2002, to March 31, 2002

Beginning Cash Balance as of 1/1/2002:		$10,000
Cash Inflows:		
Program Service Revenue:	$40,000	
Grants and Contracts:	100,000	
Interest Income:	1,000	
Total Cash Inflow from All Sources:		$141,000
Beginning Balance Plus Cash Inflows:		$151,000
Cash Disbursements:		
Salaries	$(45,000)	
Fringe Benefits:	(10,000)	
Rent:	(5,000)	
Insurance:	(1,000)	
Capital Expenditures:	(6,000)	
Loan Repayments:	(3,000)	
Total Cash Disbursements:		$(70,000)
Ending Cash Balance as of 3/31/2002:		$81,000

program service revenue, grants and contracts, and interest income. At the bottom of this section of the report, leave room for the sum of cash from all sources.

The next section of the report, the cash disbursements section, shows how cash is used. This section should be placed below the cash receipts section and should include all cash disbursements, listing them by category. Common categories for cash disbursements are rent, insurance, salaries, capital expenditures, and loan repayments. As with the cash inflow section, leave room at the bottom of this section to show the total of all disbursements.

The very bottom of the report should show net cash received or disbursed. The beginning cash balance should be placed above the cash receipts section, and the ending cash balance should be placed below the cash disbursements section. This will produce an ending cash balance that either will or will not be within an acceptable range. If current or future cash balances are below required levels, it is the organization's responsibility and duty to take corrective action to resolve the cash shortfalls. Exhibits A.1 and A.3 in Resource A are examples of additional reports one organization chose to use in monitoring cash receipts and disbursements.

B. Variance Reports

Variance reports can also assist your organization in identifying where problems may exist. A variance report compares forecasted cash flow with actual cash flow, once these data are obtained. The difference between the forecasted and actual numbers is the *variance.* Obviously, all significant variances should be investigated and explained. The variance report, like any tool, can be both under- and overused. If the report is not generated or is ignored, significant problems may go unidentified and will not be addressed in a timely manner. However, if the report is overused, valuable time and resources may be wasted on researching immaterial variances. Those responsible for cash flow monitoring must carefully select and use variance reports in the appropriate context. Universal Nonprofit's experience, as described in the following example, illustrates appropriate and beneficial use of variance reports.

Universal Nonprofit's Use of Variance Reports

Universal Nonprofit was having significant cash flow problems. Actual cash flow had been significantly lower than forecasted. We discovered that a larger-than-anticipated amount of money was being spent on personnel. Further investigation revealed that several departments in the organization were using per-diem staff hired from agencies that supplied temporary staff. The organization took this action because, as a result of recruitment problems, it had a shortage of full-time staff. Paying for the higher-priced temporary staff was leading to greater-than-expected personnel costs. Once management identified the problem through reviewing its variance reports, corrective action could be taken. Universal Nonprofit addressed the problem by launching an intensive and well-planned recruitment effort to hire full-time staff. During the following budget-planning meeting, Universal Nonprofit redesigned its approach to professional staffing, cutting its personnel costs by 15 percent.

We consider three types of variance reports to be the most useful in providing information for cash flow monitoring and modification purposes. These reports help an organization to recognize problems in operations and in the forecasting process. The three reports are the following:

1. Forecasted-versus-actual report

2. Analysis of key variances report

3. Historical variances report

1. Forecasted-Versus-Actual Report

The forecasted-versus-actual report will compare the forecasted cash flow with actual cash flow. The difference between the forecasted and actual amounts is the variance. When it is a *material* amount, the variance should be examined to determine its cause.

Materiality

Materiality is a challenging concept because a number of factors will influence the amount at which a variance is material for your particular organization. If your working capital is weak and you only have enough working capital to exist for two months, your materiality factor is going to be different from that of an organization with a twelve-month reserve of working capital. We think a good rule of thumb is to use 3 percent variance as a starting point for materiality, with 5 percent variance as a trigger for concern. In the beginning of a fiscal year, a larger variance may be better tolerated than it will be later in a fiscal year because there will still be time to correct the problem.

A forecasted-versus-actual cash flow report is an excellent tool for an organization to use in order to determine where cash flow problems exist. It is best used in conjunction with the other cash flow report mentioned earlier. See Exhibit 7.2 for an example of a forecasted-versus-actual cash flow report.

2. Analysis of Key Variances Report

The analysis of key variances report is similar to the forecasted-versus-actual report but goes into greater detail to investigate the significant variances. This report is divided into three parts. The left-hand column shows the forecasted cash flow; the second column shows the actual cash flow; and the third column with explanation is reserved for identifying significant variances and providing explanations for those variances. The purpose of the report is to make three determinations regarding each variance:

EXHIBIT 7.2	Sample Forecasted-Versus-Actual Cash Flow Report

Universal Nonprofit
Forecasted-Versus-Actual Cash Flow Report
Fiscal Year 2000

	FORECASTED CASH FLOW	ACTUAL CASH FLOW	DOLLAR VARIANCE	PERCENTAGE VARIANCE
CASH INFLOWS:				
Program Revenue	$175,000	$157,550	$(17,450)	−9.97
Grants and Contracts	575,000	550,000	(25,000)	−4.35
Contributions	75,000	95,000	20,000	26.67
Total Cash Inflows	$825,000	$802,550	$(22,450)	−2.72
CASH OUTFLOWS:				
Personnel Costs	$475,000	$481,250	$6,250	1.32
Supplies	115,000	105,125	(9,875)	−8.59
Insurance	45,000	43,500	(1,500)	−3.33
Communications	17,500	16,730	(770)	−4.40
Space Costs	150,000	152,500	2,500	1.67
Total Cash Outflows	$802,500	$799,105	$(3,395)	−0.42
NET CASH FLOW	$22,500	$3,445	$(19,055)	−84.69

Note: Even though this organization forecasted a $22,500 cash surplus, it was still able to create an actual $3,445 cash surplus by cutting cash outflows $3,395 below forecasted. By careful monitoring and increasing contributions significantly (by $20,000), it was able to overcome cash inflow shortfalls of $17,450 in program revenue and $25,000 in grant and contract revenue. It changed its game plan and had a positive cash year. This was good cash flow management. See Exhibit 7.3 for a more detailed analysis.

1. What caused the variance

2. Whether the cause of the variance was internal or external

3. How the variance will affect future cash flow forecasts, budgets, and operations

When the variance and its causes are identified, the organization must implement a corrective action plan to rectify the problem. If the source of the problem is external, an evaluation must be performed on the external factors that caused the variance, to identify any future problems. When external factors are causing ongoing problems, restructuring may be necessary to ensure the organization remains competitive in the future. For example, if a government program in which your organization participates is suddenly eliminated, your organization will have to determine how it will need to modify operations in response to this change. See Exhibits 7.3 and 7.4 for examples of analysis of key variances reports.

EXHIBIT
7.3
Sample Annual Analysis of Key Variances Report

Universal Nonprofit
Analysis of Key Variances Report
Fiscal Year 2000

	FORECASTED CASH FLOW	ACTUAL CASH FLOW	DOLLAR VARIANCE	PERCENTAGE VARIANCE	IS THE VARIANCE SIGNIFICANT?	VARIANCE ANALYSIS
CASH INFLOWS:						
Program Revenue	$175,000	$157,550	$(17,450)	−9.97	Yes	Forced to close for a week owing to severe weather.
Grants and Contracts	575,000	550,000	(25,000)	−4.35	Yes	A funding source ceased operations.
Contributions	75,000	95,000	20,000	26.67	Yes	Additional donations solicited to help offset lost grant.
Total Cash Inflows	$825,000	$802,550	$(22,450)	−2.72	Yes	See previous variance analyses.
CASH OUTFLOWS:						
Personnel Costs	$475,000	$481,250	$6,250	1.32	No	N/A
Supplies	115,000	105,125	(9,875)	−8.59	Yes	Delayed purchases.
Insurance	45,000	43,500	(1,500)	−3.33	No	Negotiated a less expensive premium.
Communications	17,500	16,730	(770)	−4.40	No	Monitored usage more effectively.
Space Costs	150,000	152,500	2,500	1.67	No	N/A
Total Cash Outflows	$802,500	$799,105	$(3,395)	−0.42	No	N/A
Net Cash Flow	$22,500	$3,445	$(19,055)	−84.69		

EXHIBIT 7.4   Sample Year-to-Date Analysis of Key Variances Report

Universal Nonprofit
Analysis of Key Variances Report
Year to Date

Program, Unit, or Activity: _____   Analysis Period: _____

Line Item	Year-to-Date Forecasted Cash Flow	Year-to-Date Actual Cash Flow	Dollar Variance	Percentage Variance	Variance Analysis
Awards and Grants	$25,000	$—	$(25,000)	–100.00	Funding source ceased operations.
Wages and Salaries	10,000	9,100	900	9.00	To date, two positions vacant; expected to be filled in June.
Payroll Taxes	10,000	8,700	1,300	13.00	See wages and salaries' variance analysis.
Travel	9,000	13,770	(4,770)	–53.00	Travel during summer will be reduced.
Equipment Repairs	7,000	3,570	3,430	49.00	Few repairs have been required to date.
Building Maintenance	6,000	3,360	2,640	44.00	Expenses are running below estimates (mild winter weather).

3. Historical Variances Report

The purpose of the historical variances report is to analyze the effectiveness of the cash flow forecasting model. This report compares the forecasted amounts with actual amounts on monthly, quarterly, and annual bases and identifies items that have been consistently forecasted incorrectly. By using this report, your organization can improve its forecasting model in order to set more realistic goals and objectives. Your organization must make sure that it clearly identifies who is responsible for the analysis of cash flow and who is responsible for supervising implementation of the corrective action plan. See Exhibit 7.5 for an example of a historical variances report. (In addition, Exhibit A.7 in Resource A shows a form useful for variance analysis.)

EXHIBIT 7.5 Sample Historical Variances Report

ABC Nonprofit
Historical Variances Report
Fiscal Year 2000

	MONTH ENDED 12/31/00			QUARTER ENDED 12/31/00			FISCAL YEAR ENDED 12/31/00		
	FORECASTED CASH FLOW	ACTUAL CASH FLOW	VARIANCE	FORECASTED CASH FLOW	ACTUAL CASH FLOW	VARIANCE	FORECASTED CASH FLOW	ACTUAL CASH FLOW	VARIANCE
CASH INFLOWS:									
Program Revenue	$27,500	$27,900	$400	$87,587	$89,280	$1,693	$360,000	$315,000	$(45,000)
Grants and Contracts	—	—	—	75,000	68,450	(6,550)	325,000	312,500	(12,500)
Contributions	15,000	15,750	750	47,775	50,400	2,625	200,000	165,000	(35,000)
Total Cash Inflows	$42,500	$43,650	$1,150	$210,362	$208,130	$(2,232)	$885,000	$792,500	$(92,500)
CASH OUTFLOWS:									
Personnel Costs	$25,000	$23,735	$(1,265)	$95,000	$107,730	$12,730	$612,500	$585,000	$(27,500)
Supplies	5,000	4,350	(650)	17,500	14,000	(3,500)	82,500	97,250	14,750
Insurance	750	800	50	2,250	2,400	150	9,750	12,500	2,750
Communications	500	515	15	1,500	1,575	75	9,000	11,250	2,250
Space Costs	10,500	10,750	250	31,500	33,000	1,500	150,000	135,000	(15,000)
Total Cash Outflows	$41,750	$40,150	$(1,600)	$147,750	$158,705	$10,955	$863,750	$841,000	$(22,750)
Net Cash Flow	$750	$3,500	$2,750	$62,612	$49,425	$(13,187)	$21,250	$(48,500)	$(69,750)

8 Strategies for Improving Cash Flow Management

Cash flow management is much more complex than just properly using budgeting methods, improving efficiency, or implementing a new billing system. Cash flow management will only be successful in the long run if it has at its foundation sound principles and thoughtfully developed strategies. In order to ensure optimal cash flow planning and management, it is often necessary for organizations to thoroughly review all areas of cash flow operations so that they can identify areas that need improvement. Once this is accomplished, organizations can then research strategies for improving cash flow in the identified areas. Finally, once the appropriate cash flow improvement strategies are chosen, they must be implemented and monitored properly.

The cash flow improvement effort cannot be confined to the realm of executive staff. It must involve the entire organization at all levels and must be considered in daily activities. This will include training managers on new techniques and approaches to their departments' cash flow responsibilities and encouraging them to explain the importance of improving cash flow to all staff members. Training sessions should be held with the goal of explaining cash flow and introducing cash flow policies. Then meetings should be held to instruct managers on the merits of policies that are geared toward increasing cash flow. Finally, meetings should be held to communicate the specific changes in each department and emphasize how the strategic approaches will improve the organization as a whole. Following these sessions, additional training sessions should be arranged to identify progress, weaknesses, and any corrective actions needed.

In this chapter, we provide strategic suggestions for improving cash flow–related operations in many areas. Obviously, not all of these suggestions will be relevant or appropriate for all organizations. We have divided the chapter into sections addressing each of the following aspects of strategic cash flow optimization:

- Income improvement strategies
- Working capital, liquidity, and financial flexibility strategies
- Investment strategies
- Banking strategies
- General cash flow improvement strategies

- Solutions for short-term negative cash flow problems
- Solutions for serious cash flow problems
- Effective ongoing cash flow management
- Special topics on cash flow improvement

A. Income Improvement Strategies

As we have stated several times throughout this book (and will continue to state because it is so crucial), organizations that are not economically successful stand little chance of having effective cash flow. The best cash flow improvement strategies will not save your organization from failing if it is routinely spending more money than it is taking in and cannot figure out how to change this. Having a sound budgeting process in place is essential to improving the financial status of your organization (see Chapter Five for information on using operating budgets in cash flow management). Accurate operating budgets that are based on sound strategic planning create the framework for an economically successful and vibrant organization. Ongoing budget monitoring will also reveal exactly which areas of your organization's financial operations need to be modified to make it even more economically successful. These concepts are the foundation of effective cash flow management.

Although these concepts sound quite simple, we have found that they are often overlooked by nonprofit organizations. In our experience one of the reasons some organizations have not afforded budgeting and cash flow management the importance or respect it deserves is because of long-held "traditions." This seems to happen most often in organizations that are or have been primarily funded by cost reimbursement grants. For these organizations, as long as grant requirements were met, funds would be received and would be sufficient to support operations. Often there would be no funds for creative projects or to use as seed money for new programs, mainly because organizations believed that all money taken in during a given year had to be spent that same year. Having a surplus somehow sent a negative message—perhaps that the organization was not doing all it should be doing to serve its purpose. These issues were a part of the problem for Universal Nonprofit. Although our model organization enjoyed sources of income other than cost reimbursement grants, the moneys it received from this source were enough to support bare-bones operations. Thus the idea of generating additional income, even through more effective management of present income sources, was not a priority.

Organizations that are primarily funded by cost reimbursement grants (usually government funds) are "intellectually" correct in terms of understanding that the type of income they receive, by its nature, *cannot* create a surplus (funds that are not used for "cost reimbursement" must be returned or, with funding source approval, used in the following fiscal period). However, it is possible in this situation for an organization to raise a small amount of money from a new revenue stream, such as a special event or a contribution drive, to create a non–cost reimbursement source of revenue.

If there is one message we would like to impart in these pages, it is that having a surplus (in a non–cost reimbursement situation) is okay. In fact, it is *good*. Having a surplus is important in keeping organizations vibrant, with funds available for innovation in creating new programs and projects. We think organizations should have a line for profit or surplus in their budgets. When organizations adopt this strategic objective and can sell their boards and staff on it, creating an effective cash flow environment will be much easier. (Part Three incorporates many practical ideas and strategies for improving cash flow through improving strategic financial management.)

B. Working Capital, Liquidity, and Financial Flexibility Strategies

This section explains the concept of working capital and the importance of maintaining adequate working capital in order to sustain liquidity and financial flexibility.

1. Working Capital

Maintaining appropriate levels of working capital and liquid assets has a greater direct effect on cash flow than any other aspect of financial operations. Organizations must understand that working capital and liquidity issues are of key importance to overall financial health. *Working capital* is defined as total current assets less total current liabilities. *Current assets* are assets that are in the form of cash or can be converted into cash within twelve months. This includes cash, inventory, accounts receivable, short-term investments, and other salable items. *Current liabilities* are liabilities that must be paid within one year. The difference between these two amounts is working capital. Exhibit 8.1 is an example of a working capital analysis for a small organization.

To make the data in Exhibit 8.1 more relevant to cash flow management, further analysis is necessary. Let us assume the organization in that example has a total budget of $1,560,000, which translates into the organization needing an average weekly inflow of $30,000 to support itself. Using the working capital figure calculated in Exhibit 8.1 ($150,000), the organization would be able to survive for five weeks without any incoming cash flow. If the organization failed to receive new cash inflow after five weeks, it would not be able to pay its staff or vendors and might be forced to go out of business. Obviously, if working capital were calculated at, for example, $300,000, the organization could survive twice as long without cash inflow. Thus whether or not an organization has appropriate working capital is a key element of overall financial health.

2. Liquidity

Liquid assets are assets that can be converted into cash in a short time and with little cost. Having liquid assets is important for organizations in order to remain solvent. Using the example in Exhibit 8.1, if the organization has cash equaling $100,000 and short-term investments that can be sold to provide another $100,000 in cash in five days, it will have enough cash to pay all liabilities except the bank loan payment. In this case, the organization would have to collect a substantial percentage of its accounts receivable to pay the bank. In many cases, banks will extend loan due dates, but sometimes they will not, which makes liquidity an ever present factor in financial management.

EXHIBIT 8.1   **Sample Working Capital Analysis**

ABC Organization
Working Capital Analysis
December 31, 2000

CURRENT ASSETS:

Cash	$100,000
Accounts Receivable	200,000
Short-Term Investments	100,000
Total Current Assets	**$400,000**

CURRENT LIABILITIES:

Accrued Payroll Expenses	$50,000
Accounts Payable	100,000
Short-Term Bank Loan (Due Within 12 Months)	100,000
Total Current Liabilities	**$250,000**

WORKING CAPITAL:

Total Current Assets	$400,000
Less Total Current Liabilities	(250,000)
Total Working Capital	**$150,000**

a. Working Capital and Liquidity Ratios. Organizations that fail to maintain adequate levels of working capital and proper liquidity risk providing lower levels of service or defaulting on their obligations. Whether with regard to for-profit or nonprofit entities, decreasing the quality or quantity of services drives consumers to the competition and makes creditors unhappy. In nonprofit organizations, lowering the levels of service can result in other problems as well, such as violation of funding agreements or contracts. In this case, the organization would be forced to find new sources of funding or to close programs. Each of these scenarios presents a serious challenge to management and is avoidable with proper planning. Proper planning includes making a commitment to focus on solvency and to maintain adequate working capital and liquidity. Doing so is part of responsible management of the organization.

The proper amount of working capital an organization should have is determined by applying standard accounting formulas and then taking into consideration the financial nature of the organization. Organizations that have less stable funding will want to keep at least six months to a year of working capital available to meet expenses if anticipated cash is not received. Organizations largely funded by federal government grants usually need less working capital. Conversely, organizations funded by local government grants may need to have more working capital to offset the potential cash flow problems sometimes associated with these funding sources.

Determining your organization's ideal amount of working capital will depend on details of the cash flow forecast. Generally, organizations should have a reasonable idea of week-to-week cash requirements, based on payroll, accounts payable, and analyses of liabilities. Having adequate liquid assets will mean that the organization will always have enough cash available to meet expected cash outflows, even during the heaviest periods of cash disbursement. When cash is not required to pay down obligations, it should be held in interest-bearing accounts to maximize the organization's return on assets.

Organizations must implement plans that call for a continual monitoring and maintenance of working capital. Setting working capital thresholds, as described previously, can preserve liquidity and solvency. The thresholds serve to function as operating guidelines that can alert management to problems in the liquidity structure. Management can then implement a corrective action plan to address any liquidity concerns.

Organizations must also use cash flow forecasts to identify any future changes in cash flow that could adversely affect liquidity. This process basically involves identifying future cash flows and both standard and special cash payments and receipts, as well as evaluating whether the organization might face any cash deficits down the line. If organizations find that they will not have enough liquid assets to cover cash outflow, corrective actions will be necessary. These may involve selling assets, reducing expenses, or increasing income.

b. Liquidity Management Strategies. Three basic steps can help organizations to better manage their liquidity. These steps are:

1. Identifying the sources of and threats to the organization's liquidity

2. Planning and forecasting future liquidity

3. Using reports to better monitor and manage liquidity

See exhibits in Chapter Seven and Part Five for various useful examples.

The process of identifying the sources of and threats to liquidity involves more than simply forecasting cash flows. It involves evaluating the organization as a whole and recognizing future commitments that could affect future ability to pay down obligations. For example, deteriorating fixed assets (such as a roof or an office building) will eventually require significant cash to repair or replace. Without proper forecasting of this issue and without adequate planning, the organization may be forced to use operating funds for capital expenditures. This is a common cash flow mistake and a dangerous one. Proper analyses must be prepared to ensure that management has an accurate understanding of the organization's true cash flow status so that it can plan accordingly for capital and other expenditures that will affect cash flow. Also, in this way, the organization will become aware in advance of potential cash flow dangers and take proactive measures.

As stated previously, organizations must also implement models to forecast future liquidity. This involves planning future cash disbursements and estimating future cash receipts. This process will provide the necessary information to form cash flow forecasts, estimate future cash balances, and take corrective actions to reverse potential deficits.

Regular and comprehensive cash flow reporting will also be essential to managing liquidity. Reports should include comparisons between actual cash flow and forecasted cash flow and should identify the margin above or below forecasted working capital.

c. Liquidity Management Challenges. Liquidity is particularly difficult to maintain in organizations that rely heavily on donor funding. Economic, social, and performance variables cause donation funding to vary significantly. Also, donor bases are more difficult to expand and require greater effort to maintain than traditional service or grant funding sources.

Management must also keep its liquidity targets in mind when examining service levels. The problem with service-oriented operation models is that increased service levels do not necessarily mean more funding. This is in contrast to a commercial retail operation, in which additional funds are generated with every item sold. For example, if a shelter serves 50 percent more meals in a week, it will not automatically receive 50 percent more funds to support the meals (unless it has this sort of arrangement with a funding source). Thus service-based organizations must be certain that their budgeted levels of service do not exceed their cash flow capacity.

Management must recognize liquidity and solvency as key parts of the organization's mission. Every organization has a service objective or mission that it must fulfill in order to be successful. If the organization fails to attend to its cash flow concerns, it will have no chance of accomplishing its service objectives or its mission.

3. Financial Flexibility

Another aspect of cash flow management that is important in overall strategic cash flow planning is flexibility and being open to alternatives. The ability to modify plans in response to environmental changes is essential to solvency and, in some cases, to the survival of your organization. The economic realities of the current public and private marketplaces demand that organizations remain flexible and constantly seek alternatives. Both government and private funding sources and investments are subject to fluctuating conditions beyond your organization's control. Our economy has evolved into a dynamic interlinked system; markets are dependent on and reactive to each other. Organizations that operate in this economy must be able to adapt to change. As an example, several major nonprofits were designated as beneficiaries of funds from a well-known philanthropic family. Recently the company founded by the donors cut the cash dividend paid on stock. A number of articles have appeared discussing the hardships now faced by the organizations that had counted on the dividend income staying the same to fund operations. Other examples: heating costs during the winter of 2000 rose considerably for many organizations; higher energy costs will have an impact on organizations in California. Such organizations had to either redo cash forecasts to accommodate the higher costs or seek out cheaper heating or energy alternatives. Situations such as these are why it is important to incorporate flexibility into as many cash flow policies and management strategies as possible.

C. Investment Strategies

This section contains some suggestions for strategies to improve cash flow related to investments.

1. Improving Investment Income

Organizations should always be exploring ways of improving returns on investments. Getting the most out of investments without a high degree of risk should be a priority. On the conservative end of the spectrum, the organization should be using *money funds* (also known as *money market funds*). Money funds are pools of invested assets, similar to mutual funds, that invest in short-term liquid assets. Well-managed money funds can provide a high degree of safety, both risks and returns vary depending on the investment mix of each individual fund. We recommend funds invested in government securities to our clients.

Organizations must assess the types of assets they are holding in order to make the most prudent investment choices. For example, long-term endowments may be managed by holding at least a portion of total assets in higher-risk equity investments. Other portions of endowments might be invested in corporate and government bonds, which are lower-risk instruments. Also, some of the endowment should be invested in a money market fund to maintain security and liquidity.

The asset allocation between high-, intermediate-, and low-risk investments is very important to ensuring optimal returns. The longer the holding period (that is, the longer until funds are required), the more risk investors can take because there is time to recover losses. Thus organizations that have long-term endowment funds or funds for capital projects that will not be used for a number of years may want to invest in a higher percentage of higher-risk instruments. Historically, the riskier the investment, the greater the return, provided the risk was warranted. Failure to properly assess risk or to balance investments can be disastrous to organizations. A major American university failed to balance its risks adequately and lost several hundred million dollars in a single investment during the 1990s.

Organizations that are actively investing their assets should strongly consider engaging a money manager who is experienced in managing nonprofit organizations' investments. Such managers, in our opinion, should be independent of brokerage houses. Professionals with a background in this area will understand the special concerns of organizations and will be able to provide the most useful and productive assistance. Most money managers charge sliding fees, which go down as the asset base increases. The fee for the first $1 million is frequently about 1 percent and can go down to 0.5 percent for assets over $10 million. However, rates vary depending on a number of factors, and organizations should have a clear idea of their investment goals before interviewing prospective money managers. We suggest that once your organization identifies its goals and priorities for investing, you conduct a formal selection process to secure the best portfolio manager for your organization.

Note

Make sure your organization's investment assets are *not* in the custody of the investment manager (unless the manager is a bank trust department). Stocks and bonds should be entrusted only to a bank or recognized brokerage firm for safekeeping.

2. Seeking Alternatives for Investments

Organizations should review alternatives for their asset allocations to ensure they are getting the best return. This is especially true in the case of endowments. Maximizing the safety and return on endowment funds will result in improved cash flow to support the purpose for which the endowment was originally created. We suggest your organization discuss with its investment adviser the following questions about its endowments:

- How much of the endowment is invested in stocks, corporate bonds, government bonds, or international stocks and bonds?

- Are the organization's assets diversified, comprising many different investments, to prevent any single investment from causing a catastrophic loss?

- What is the risk of a catastrophic loss in any of these investments?

- Are the expected returns worth the risk the organization is taking on the investments?

By asking the preceding questions, your organization can identify any undue risks it may be taking. In addition, this analysis will help organizations assess their level of flexibility and the volatility of all of their investments. Investments in money market funds and government bonds are always a safer bet because, compared with other investments, they are typically less volatile, can be more flexible, have shorter terms, and are more easily converted to liquid assets. However, the greater flexibility and lower volatility of government securities comes at a price: lower expected returns.

An aspect of investment planning that organizations frequently overlook is coordinating the type of investment with the future purpose of the invested funds. For example, we worked with an organization that had completed an unusually good capital campaign, successfully raising the $1 million it needed for expansion nine months ahead of schedule. The controller of the organization discovered what she thought was an attractive investment for the capital money. The organization's bank agreed that it was a good investment. It was a *no load* fund (that is, a commission would not be charged when the security was purchased). We visited the client a couple of weeks after the organization made its investment. The controller informed us that the start date on the project had been pushed up and that the money would be needed in six months. We read the prospectus describing the investment in detail and found a clause—not uncommon in this type of no load fund—stipulating a 2 percent commission if the security was sold within one year. Moreover, the prospectus stated that a commission would be charged unless the investment was held for at least five years. In selling the security to meet cash flow needs, our client paid a $20,000 commission. Although this particular investment might have been fine for an endowment fund, it was clearly not appropriate for funds that might be needed on short notice.

To avoid this type of situation and other potential investment mistakes, an organization should have its board's investment committee or other applicable committee review the recommendations of its investment portfolio manager on a regular basis. In addition, the performance of the manager should be evaluated against recognized standard investment indices on a regular basis.

D. Banking Strategies

This section offers suggestions for cash flow strategies related to banking.

1. Knowing Your Bank's Services

Using banking services and expertise can further enhance cash flow. Your organization should obtain an account analysis periodically to identify threats and opportunities in cash management. Perhaps the organization has been holding larger balances in its checking account than necessary.

Organizations should view banking services just as they would any other service. Many organizations do not realize they can shop around and negotiate for the best possible banking terms. Putting bank services out for bid can also be helpful in getting the best banking deal for your organization if you are located in an area with a competitive banking environment.

2. Reporting Your Bank Balance

The organization should also consider using bank balance reporting and on-line banking features. These features give management important information that will allow for more timely allocation of resources. For example, when bank balances are closely monitored, your organization can maintain the most advantageous proportion of funds in interest-bearing and non-interest-bearing accounts. Some larger organizations that have more sophisticated finance departments may opt to maintain zero checking account balances. This strategy requires an organization to move money daily from interest-bearing accounts to cover disbursements from checking accounts. In this way, the organization's cash can earn income until it is needed, instead of sitting in a non-interest-bearing checking account. After careful research and negotiation with its bank, Universal Nonprofit was able to double the interest it earned.

3. Improving Your Banking Efficiency

Making the best use of the bank in which your organization maintains its accounts can be instrumental in improving cash flow. In order to do this, you must perform a thorough analysis pf your organization's accounts, with special attention to their number, types, amount of cash, and associated fees. Once this is done, inefficiencies will become quite apparent. For example, if an organization has twenty different checking, savings, and money market accounts, cash flow will be very difficult to monitor. The administrative tasks necessary to manage redundant accounts (such as verifying balances and doing bank reconciliations) waste time and money. Further, with many separate accounts there is an increased danger of transferring funds into the wrong account or paying funds from an account that is designated for another purpose. The best strategy is to maintain the fewest number of accounts necessary to serve your organization's banking purposes.

From a control perspective, lockbox accounts are also useful in improving cash flow. Lockbox accounts work by collecting and recording cash payments that clients, donors, or funding sources send to a central location. This eliminates the problems that may surface when envelopes containing money are opened in a less secure office environment. This type of account is most useful for contribution-funded or fee-for-service-driven organizations with a large client or donor base. For example, in the case of an organization that receives many donations, establishing a lockbox account would be ideal because it would eliminate the risk of loss associated with internal personnel processing contributions. In addition, organizations that receive a large volume of funds just a few times a year usually do not have the staff to process so many transactions properly. The bank's staff can easily handle the sporadic volume and can deposit the money received into interest-bearing accounts the same day it arrives.

Multicurrency accounts allow for the receipt and payment of cash in different currencies. These accounts should be considered by organizations that regularly receive such income.

E. General Cash Flow Improvement Strategies

There are many ways management can improve cash flow in the long run. This section discusses several that have not been addressed in previous sections.

1. Improving Your Capability to Receive Funds

Organizations should make sure they are using all available cash receipt alternatives. For example, your organization should be capable of receiving electronic funds transfers and be able to process credit card payments via the Internet, fax, or telephone media.

See Chapter Ten for a detailed discussion of technology and its ability to enhance cash flow.

2. Earmarking Cash

The organization should segregate resources so that the necessary amount of cash is earmarked to pay off obligations. For example, when a grant is received by an organization to fund a program, management must identify what portion of those resources will be used to purchase supplies, pay salaries, and cover administrative costs.

F. Solutions for Short-Term Negative Cash Flow Problems

Short-term negative cash flow is different from a chronic cash flow problem. When cash flow problems are either ongoing or occur consistently, organizations must consider this a serious overall cash flow planning and management issue. Suggestions for correcting serious cash flow problems can be found throughout this book; some important ones are summarized later in this chapter.

Short-term cash flow difficulties can be the result of a number of operational or financial situations that unexpectedly arise. Unforeseen changes or delays in funding and unanticipated higher expenses are two problems that can result in negative cash flow of limited duration. Of course, a period of negative cash flow can also be the result of oversights in an area of cash flow planning or management. In addition, short-term cash flow problems can occur during "crisis" situations—unique events that cause the organization to spend more than it receives. Obviously, organizations that plan and manage cash flow effectively will have some cash reserves that can be used to meet short-term cash flow problems. Exhibit 8.2 presents some suggestions for organizations that may have exhausted reserve funds in meeting expenses and must address short-term negative cash flow in other ways.

Generally, the strategies listed in Exhibit 8.2 will not compromise an organization's mission or services. However, each of them carries potential negative consequences. For example, loans, credit, and installment plans will usually incur interest, which is an additional expense. Postponing payments to vendors might make them treat the organization less favorably in the future.

EXHIBIT 8.2   **Strategies for Addressing Short-Term Negative Cash Flow**

- Delay nonessential purchases.
- Request extensions on payments to vendors.
- Establish installment plans with vendors to pay for essential purchases.
- Postpone hiring new personnel or awarding salary increases to staff (subject to union contracts).
- Plan an "emergency" or quickly instituted fundraising drive.
- Request cash advances from funding sources.
- Seek short-term loans from banks or board members.
- Use available lines of credit.
- Transfer money from other internal accounts that may be paid back when cash flow is once again positive (subject to legal and regulatory restrictions).
- Borrow against investments.
- Engage in careful cost cutting.

Note

When organizations are having cash flow problems that make it difficult to pay vendors on time, the vendors should be informed of the situation. A well-informed creditor will usually be more cooperative than one with whom the organization does not communicate clearly and honestly.

Extreme caution should be exercised whenever transferring funds from cash accounts that may have restrictions on their use. A large health care organization had three of its senior officers indicted for alleged improper use of restricted endowment funds to compensate for cash flow problems. To avoid violating laws or contract obligations, organizations that are grant funded or that have endowments must be extra careful when using this strategy.

Holding an emergency fundraising drive also has its risks. Organizations that make such an appeal to donors might generate a lack of confidence in the organization's ability to manage itself effectively. Finally, postponing staff salary increases might hurt morale, as will delays in hiring additional staff when current staff is overburdened.

Cost cutting, as mentioned elsewhere in this book, can also be detrimental to operations if not performed with due care. In addressing short-term negative cash flow problems, the type of cost cutting we suggest only includes strategies that would have minimal effects on your organization's operations. Extreme cost-cutting measures should never be employed unless absolutely necessary.

G. Solutions for Serious Cash Flow Problems

When organizations consistently face negative cash flow situations, the best action they can take is to reconsider and reorganize their overall cash flow management approach. However, if your organization faces a serious cash flow problem for which extreme measures are the only solution, it may be forced to try the following strategies:

- *Reduce staff by eliminating positions, not filling vacated positions, or modifying plans to hire new staff.* Layoffs and salary reductions can also be used to improve cash flow. Some organizations have successfully reduced staff workweeks as an alternative to staff layoffs. Organizations that can implement this strategy are more likely to retain their trained staff as employees. Once operations return to normal, staff can be allowed to return to full-time employment. This may help maintain staff morale, as everyone is sharing some of the pain yet no one is being terminated.

- *Postpone starting or expanding new activities or programs.*

- *Reduce services or eliminate a program or activity that is not cost effective.*

Note

Cost reimbursement–funded organizations must be careful when modifying services, staff, or programs, as cost reimbursement funding will be reduced commensurately to the cost reductions.

Keep in mind that each of these strategies can result in the organization compromising its mission or service provision and should only be considered when there are no other viable alternatives. Organizations that must resort to significant cuts in programs or services should thoroughly review all funding source and regulatory requirements to ensure that no contract provisions or regulations are being violated. Moreover, organizations should be prepared for the adverse effects such actions might have on their public image and trustworthiness to clients and funding sources.

See Chapter Fourteen for more information on grant income.

H. Effective Ongoing Cash Flow Management

This section provides some suggestions for overall planning for effective cash flow management.

1. Setting and Meeting Cash Flow Targets

First, the organization must forecast future cash flow targets and determine how readily achievable these targets are. Next, the organization must identify its major cash management activities. Cash collection is probably one of the most significant cash management activities in terms of improving cash flow. The organization must assess whether any significant changes can be made to boost collection success. Examples of such modifications are new billing systems or tighter internal controls (both of these issues are covered in Chapters Three and Eleven).

2. Analyzing Cash Flow Plans

The next step in planning cash flow is analyzing cash disbursements to determine if there are any ways to limit the amount of cash outflow.

After a thorough review of all cash flow considerations, the organization can begin cash planning and forecasting. The cash-forecasting activities should focus on the review of projected cash balances. Following the review, management should address any cash shortages based on these projections.

With this information available, management can develop a better understanding of how to optimize cash flow. After expected cash inflow and outflow are thoroughly reviewed, and modified as needed, an accurate and detailed cash flow forecast can be developed. This forecast will be the basis for all cash flow–related decisions in the future.

In addition, the cash flow planning and the budgeting process should include an analysis of changes in assumptions. For example, how would cash flow be affected if interest rates rose by 0.50 or 0.75 percent? How would cash flow for a donor supported organization be affected by a recession or severe drop in stock markets? Organizations should also review vendor, funding-source, government, and contributor demands to determine how changes in these areas could affect cash flow planning. Each of these parties may have restrictive rules that could hinder the organization's cash flow flexibility. Examples of such rules include maintaining a certain percentage of investments in money market accounts, achieving a predetermined liquidity level, or providing a predetermined level of service. Organizations should also conduct periodic reviews of the credit markets to remain aware of credit availability and the cost of obtaining funds.

I. Special Topics on Cash Flow Improvement

1. Cutting Employee Costs

As mentioned elsewhere in this book, employee costs often consume the largest share of the budget of nonprofit organizations. Thus any effort to reduce expenses and improve cash flow must include a review of personnel-related cash outflows. The objectives of such a review are threefold:

1. To determine if staffing levels are structured to be as efficient as possible and to research cost-cutting alternatives

2. To determine if current fringe benefits offered to staff are appropriate for the organization and are economically feasible

3. To gather information to use in planning for modifications that will increase employee efficiency and to implement such modifications

a. Assessing Efficiency in Staffing. Organizations should review the following aspects of staffing to determine if cash flow may be improved with modifications:

- **Redundancy and Overstaffing.** Are there any areas or functions in the organization for which there is redundancy among staff members? Are there any functions that might be performed by fewer staff members than currently deployed for these functions? Can any functions in individual departments or units be consolidated with similar functions in other departments or units so that fewer staff members are needed to perform the functions? Would it make sense to form a clerical pool instead of providing each executive with individual clerical support?

- **Organizational Restructuring.** Are there any ways in which the hierarchical structure of the organization might be modified to increase employee and overall operational efficiency? (Some organizations have successfully eliminated a level of supervision by giving staff more responsibility at the point of service. Training staff to assume management responsibilities has resulted in as much as a 15 percent reduction in direct service costs in some organizations with which we have worked. Moreover, client satisfaction can increase substantially when staff possesses better management skills.)

- **Outsourcing.** Are there any functions currently performed by employees that might be performed more economically if outsourced?

- **Consultants and Independent Contractors.** Are there any functions or roles for which hiring consultants or independent contractors would be more economical than maintaining salaried employees?

b. Reviewing Employee Benefits. Organizations should examine the following aspects of the benefits they currently offer to employees:

- **Offering Adequate Benefits.** Are employee benefits packages competitive with those of organizations in the same field of service and geographical area, and of the same size and structure? Are benefits packages either overly generous or substandard, in terms of benefits offered and associated premiums or contributions expected from employees?

- **Getting the Most Economical Benefits.** Have alternative benefit providers and benefit plans been researched to determine if current benefits are the most economical? Has the organization looked into existing options for health, disability, workers' compensation, life insurance, cafeteria plans, retirement benefits, deferred compensation plans, and so on?

c. Planning and Implementing Modifications to Employee-Related Expenses. Organizations that have reviewed employee-related expenses and have found areas that need modification to improve cash flow should take the following steps:

1. Have the CEO, CFO, and director of human resources meet to discuss, review, and develop an action plan.

2. Approve and finalize the action plan.

3. Have the CEO, CFO, or director of human resources meet with department and unit heads to announce the action plan and assign responsibilities in the modification process.

4. Implement the modifications.

5. Generate progress reports at biweekly intervals.

6. Evaluate the success of the action plan in terms of improving cash flow.

2. Issuing Bonds

One strategy for improving cash flow some organizations might consider is using bond-based financing methods for a project or program. This form of financing must be examined very carefully to determine whether the necessary elements exist to support a bond offering and whether such an offering would be practical. The first consideration in bond financing is understanding how the payments on the bond should be made. Debt repayment must come from new sources of funding, such as program revenues. For example, if a church is planning to build a new day-care center with bond financing, it must be able to document that increased revenues will allow the bond principal and interest to be paid.

Organizations researching bond-financing options must also consider what the bond proceeds will be applied toward. An inappropriate bond issue can lead to higher than necessary costs of borrowing and to bondholder lawsuits. For example, if the organization will use the funds to construct new buildings or acquire property, a *mortgage bond* will be the type of bond to be researched. A mortgage bond is a certain type of bond issued to investors that is secured by the real estate purchased with the funds. If the organization defaults on the bond issue, the investors may lay claim to the real estate and liquidate it to obtain the funds they are owed. However, if the organization will be using the bond's proceeds for general start-up costs and the acquisition or development of intangible assets, offering a *revenue bond* may be more suitable. A revenue bond will allow the investors to have a claim on the future revenues of the organization. Thus if the organization defaults on these bonds, the investors may lay claim to the revenue of the organization to obtain the funds they are owed. For all of these reasons, we strongly advise that organizations engage the services of a qualified and experienced consultant when considering bond financing. Issuing bonds is a complex method of financing and often too expensive for smaller organizations. However, most states have special bond authorities that will assist organizations in creating a bond issue.

3. Using Debt as a Corrective Action

Organizations may find themselves in need of a corrective action plan in light of current or forecasted cash flow deficiencies. When this scenario is primarily the result of cash flow timing, a short-term loan or a line of credit should be used to allow the organization to continue operations in an efficient manner. However, if the cash flow deficiency is related to operational shortcomings, the organization must design a more operations-focused plan of corrective action. This plan would include changes in the structure, strategy, and operation of the organization rather than merely implementation of a financing arrangement. Although borrowing funds during the period of correction may be required, it should not be undertaken lightly or as a way of addressing a more serious operational problem (such as losing money from operations). Unfortunately, we have seen organizations try to borrow their way out of cash flow problems without adequately addressing the underlying operational problems.

4. Reducing UBIT Liability

Nonprofits that derive income from activities that are not related to their tax-exempt purposes may be subject to UBIT on those earnings. Furthermore, organizations that earn too much UBI jeopardize their tax exempt status. See Exhibit 8.3 for definitions of UBI.

In reality, there are only a small number of organizations that have to pay UBIT, and it is highly unusual for a nonprofit organization to have its tax-exempt status challenged for UBI-related reasons. This is because many of the income-generating activities in which nonprofits may engage are excluded from consideration as UBI. The IRS has listed forty exclusion categories into which an overwhelming majority of nonprofit business operations will fall. In addition, there are steps (that are both legal and ethical) that many organizations can take to make sure their economic activities fall into an exclusion category. Organizations that end up with UBIT liability will have to factor UBIT payments into their cash flow planning and management. The following subsections list several strategies for reducing or eliminating UBIT liability.

| EXHIBIT 8.3 | Definition of Unrelated Business Income |

Income earned from business activities "substantially related" to a nonprofit's tax-exempt purpose are not subject to UBIT. Business activities carried out by nonprofits that are considered to be unrelated will generate UBI if all of the following are true:

1. The income is from a trade or business regularly carried on by the organization.
2. The activity itself is not substantially related to carrying out the organization's exempt purpose (regardless of what is eventually done with the income).
3. The activity or its income is not excluded from taxation, primarily under Internal Revenue Code sections 512, 513, and 514.

a. Using Volunteer Staffing. Organizations that conduct business operations using a volunteer workforce may completely avoid paying UBIT, even when such activities are unrelated to the nonprofit's tax-exempt purpose. Furthermore, the amount of income that may be earned tax free in this manner is without limitation. For example, one of the best-known charities in the United States earns millions of dollars a year selling donated items and does not pay a cent of UBIT. This is in spite of the fact that selling goods does not "contribute importantly" to the organization's exempt purpose, except in providing income. The reason the income from the sales is not subject to UBIT is that all sales-related operations are carried out almost entirely by a volunteer labor force.

b. Modifying Your Organization's IRS Tax-Exempt Purpose. Nonprofits that earn substantial UBI and do not meet other criteria for exemption from paying UBIT do have another tax avoidance option. Organizations may modify the tax-exempt purpose they stated in their original IRS application for exemption. An organization that is conducting a business activity that is not "substantially related" to its current reason for exemption can notify the IRS that a new activity is being contemplated and explain how it is related to the organization's exempt purpose.

Here is an example of how an organization can use this strategy to exempt income from UBIT:

A nonprofit for which the exempt purpose is providing school-year enrichment services started offering summer tutoring services. Soon thereafter it became apparent that many parents in the community were interested in a summer recreation camp for their children. The nonprofit developed a summer camp program that became very popular and successful. The summer camp now provides income to the nonprofit. If the organization wants to avoid paying UBIT on the earned income, it can amend its tax-exempt purpose by adding "summer enrichment and exercise" to it. Of course, this would be subject to acceptance of the concept by the IRS.

Organizations considering modification of their exempt purpose should consult attorneys and accountants experienced in this area before taking any actions.

c. Forming a For-Profit Subsidiary. Organizations that earn enough UBI that it comprises a large proportion of their total income risk losing their tax-exempt status. Regardless of how much UBIT such organizations are willing to pay and no matter what their exempt purpose, the IRS limits the amount of UBI an organization may earn before questioning its tax-exempt status. (Unfortunately, there are no actual numbers or proportions offered by the IRS to define "too much" UBI. However, UBI as 50 percent of total income could conceivably fall into that category.) Nonprofits that have no other options in terms of avoiding UBIT on their business income may want to consider forming a for-profit subsidiary. The for-profit then assumes all of the business activities and pays the corporate tax rate on income. The nonprofit continues to perform the activities and functions that fulfill its tax-exempt purpose without any risk to its exemption. UBIT is equivalent to the corporate tax rate, so the related organizations do not pay any more income taxes than the nonprofit would have if it had retained its business activities. However, the nonprofit also ensures that its main reason for existing is not questioned.

Forming a separate for-profit corporation can offer a number of other benefits, such as:

- Protecting the nonprofit from possible liability or other problems that could arise in generating UBI

- Segregating the income and expenses connected with unrelated business activities, thus providing a clearer picture of the value of the unrelated business activity

- Eliminating the need to analyze and allocate the nonprofit's income and expenses between related and unrelated business activities

Not all nonprofits generating substantial UBI will be best served by creating a for-profit subsidiary. To determine whether or not this option is a viable one, your organization should consider the following factors:

- Will your nonprofit produce or potentially produce enough UBI to raise the possibility of jeopardizing tax-exempt status?

- Is the nature of the unrelated business activity substantially different from the related activities of the nonprofit? For example, does it require special equipment, separate facilities, specialized staff, and so on?

- Is excessive record keeping necessary to segregate unrelated business activities, to keep separate accounts for direct expenses, to allocate expenses, and so on?

If your organization answers one or more of these questions in the affirmative, we suggest a consultation with an experienced financial professional to determine whether or not your organization would benefit from having a for-profit subsidiary.

d. Avoiding UBI from Debt-Financed Property. If your organization earns income from property that is partially or completely debt financed, such income may be subject to UBIT. Obviously, the best way to avoid this situation is to plan properly so that debt financing is kept to a minimum on income-earning property. This is a situation in which effective strategic and capital planning truly pay off. Organizations that can raise funds and develop effective long-term strategic plans and effective capital budgets will be able to buy income-producing property outright and therefore avoid paying UBIT. However, this entire area of taxation has a number of variables, so calculating taxes owed, if any, can be a tricky endeavor, and it is best left to a professional tax adviser.

CHAPTER 9

Cash Flow Planning and Budgeting for Capital Projects

Cash flow planning and budgeting for capital projects are essential for the sustained financial health of most organizations. The process of planning, evaluating, and acquiring assets for long-term use is an important yet frequently misunderstood aspect of effective cash flow management. Because capital projects often involve purchases of costly assets, such as land, buildings, and major equipment, they generally have a substantial and lasting impact. This impact can be either positive or negative, depending on the effectiveness of capital budgeting and cash flow planning processes. Organizations contemplating a capital project should make sure that enough time and resources are devoted to an adequate preparation phase. In most cases, this will involve researching the prospective capital project, deciding on the best time to initiate the project, and determining how the project will be financed. Organizations that fail to consider each of these aspects of capital cash flow planning and capital budgeting risk making poor decisions. These poor decisions can affect the organization's cash flow and overall financial health for many years to come.

The most important aspect of capital cash flow planning and budgeting concerns the way major purchases will be financed. Financing requires careful economic analyses of alternative methods for obtaining the needed resources. However, these analyses are only appropriate in situations when the expenditures are large enough to justify the time and effort. Your organization should choose a threshold dollar amount at which a purchase becomes a "capital" item. Purchases that meet the threshold should be analyzed to determine the best financing approach. Moreover, this type of transaction should trigger additional approval or decision-making steps (such as board committee approval) that must be taken before making the purchase. Federal government accounting rules usually differentiate between an *expense* (under $5,000) and a *capital item* ($5,000 and over). Your organization must determine what its trigger point will be for defining a capital purchase.

Some organizations approach capital project planning and budgeting by creating capital budgets covering five years of anticipated capital needs. This sort of plan establishes a clear perspective on the financing alternatives available. Of course, all capital project decision making should be based on the organization's mission, goals, and objectives. Cash flow forecasts and program requirements are also essential data in developing capital project plans and budgets.

Organizations that are seeking to finance a capital project must closely scrutinize all of the cash flow ramifications of any financing agreement. Adverse environmental factors and scenarios should be considered in the context of their impact on the organization's flexibility. Your organization must reject any financing agreement that jeopardizes its fiscal health or ability to further its mission and objectives.

We strongly recommend that all organizations considering a capital project establish a capital budget planning committee. This committee should comprise a cross section of the organization's staff, including finance, accounting, and operations personnel, and should be responsible for guiding the organization's capital planning, budgeting, and financing. Ineffective capital budgeting is extremely dangerous to cash flow. Your organization's capital cash flow planning and budgeting process must protect your organization from the risks associated with capital projects.

If your organization is planning to finance a capital project with debt, as opposed to contributions or grants, you must determine how the debt will be repaid. Your repayment plan must be completed and analyzed before your organization borrows any money. For example, if your nonprofit is borrowing money to fund an equipment purchase for a transportation program benefiting the homebound elderly, you should be able to document how your organization will repay the lender after taking into consideration the additional costs of operating the program.

Capital budgeting must be tied into overall budget planning in order to be successful. Unfortunately, some organizations fail to coordinate their budgeting and cash flow planning in this manner. In our experience we have found that this can be a serious oversight. Your organization can run a successful capital campaign and build a facility but then have inadequate funds to staff and furnish the facility or do the proper marketing. Capital budgets must be carefully coordinated with operational planning in order to avoid this situation.

In the example just cited, the capital budget should have included money for the equipment necessary to furnish the new facility and for marketing the facility to the community. In addition, the operating budget should have been coordinated with the capital budget and cash flow forecasts so that the project could be properly implemented. Institutions that fund capital projects, such as banks, understand these issues and will lend money for marketing and equipment. However, organizations must have effective capital and operational budgets and cash flow forecasts in order to identify and convey their funding needs.

This chapter provides suggestions and information regarding the various aspects of developing effective cash flow planning and budgeting processes for capital projects.

A. Evaluating Your Organization's Operating Environment

The operating environment of the organization will have a significant impact on the types of projects or programs the organization can and should pursue. Obviously, the organization's current and anticipated financial health will figure prominently in capital project decision making. Other operational factors that should be thoroughly evaluated when considering a capital project are the following:

- **Personnel Needs.** Does your organization have, on its staff or board, people with the necessary skills, experience, and availability to research, implement, and manage the capital project?

- **Necessary Resources.** When all relevant expenses (for example, consultant fees, legal fees, and up-front financing costs) are taken into account, does your organization have the financial and personnel resources to research and implement a capital project without compromising cash flow?

- **Support of Your Mission.** Does the capital project under consideration support the organization's mission and tax-exempt purpose?

- **Relationship to Other Activities.** How does the capital project fit in with other activities being conducted by the organization? How will implementing such a project support, detract from, or otherwise affect current programs and activities?

- **Community Support.** How is the community likely to react to the capital project under consideration? Will it be necessary to build support? Does the community stand to gain from the project? (Obtaining this information may allow organizations to engage in a larger project than they would otherwise. Certain government "enrichment" programs will help organizations finance projects that address community needs in the areas of housing, health, and economic development.)

B. Evaluating Economic Variables

Economic variables will have a large effect on decisions to implement a capital project and on later capital project cash flow and capital budgeting. The rate of inflation, interest rates, and consumer sentiment will all be important factors in evaluating capital projects. When engaged in the financing process, it is important not only to understand the economic reality now but also to understand where the economy is going. For example, current and forecasted interest rates will be critical information in making financing decisions. The higher the interest rate at which the organization obtains financing, the more cash flow must be generated to pay the financing costs.

Inflation is also an important factor in capital cash flow planning because the greater the rate of inflation, the greater future cash outflow will be to pay for increases in the price of supplies and services. This will make it necessary to generate more income in order to fund projects and programs. In addition, the role of consumer sentiment in making capital project decisions cannot be overlooked. Organizations must gauge the current trends in the public's willingness to make charitable contributions. For example, in times of economic expansion and prosperity, people are more generous because they have more to give and are less anxious about their own economic futures. However, in times of economic retrenchment or recession, consumers may be less likely to give to charitable organizations. Therefore if the economic forecasts predict higher inflation, higher interest rates, and decreasing consumer confidence, these factors must be given due consideration in determining whether or not to pursue a particular project or program.

C. Evaluating Capital Projects

After the organization's operating environment and economic variables have been evaluated, the next phase of capital cash flow planning and budgeting involves evaluating the programs or projects under consideration. This step may be relatively simple and quick or may involve extensive research, depending on the exact project. Obviously, the evaluation process will be quite different for a capital project that involves only the purchase of a vehicle than it will be for a project that involves purchasing land on which to build new facilities. Organizations must make sure that they are realistic in budgeting enough resources and time to evaluate the particular type of capital project they are contemplating. This will entail gaining an understanding of the relevant marketplace and becoming familiar with all that is associated with such a venture.

Evaluating a capital project involves four steps:

Step 1   Composing a list of projects

Step 2   Reviewing each project for feasibility

Step 3   Forecasting cash flows

Step 4   Determining the true economic cost of the project

Each of these steps is discussed in the subsections that follow.

1. Composing a List of Projects

The goal in evaluating potential capital projects is to select the projects that will use the organization's funds in the most productive manner. The first step in the evaluation is to compose a list of projects for consideration. The list should also include alternatives, such as setting up a complex project or program as several separate and independent projects. For each project on the list, your organization should create a detailed description including operational expenses related to the project—such as staff salaries, utility costs, supplier costs—any capital asset needs, future growth expectations, and other information pertinent to developing a cost analysis. While compiling the information for each project, keep in mind that projections of capital purchases should include costs related to transportation, installation, approval by local authorities, and any other costs associated with developing or implementing the capital project. Again, depending on the source of funds, your organization may be able to include costs in addition to construction in the capital budget if they are incurred during a startup period; for example, equipment and marketing costs.

2. Reviewing Each Project for Feasibility

Each project should be reviewed for its feasibility and how well it supports the organization's mission. A project that immediately seems too costly or extravagant may need to be reconsidered. In such a case, organizations should examine alternative ways of accomplishing the project's goal. For example, some complex or expensive projects might work well as part of a joint venture. Projects that are not aligned with the organization's mission may present a host of problems and should be seriously reevaluated. After reconsideration, if the project still remains compelling, the organization might consider modifying its mission or entering into a joint venture with another organization to implement the project.

3. Forecasting Cash Flows

The third phase in evaluating a capital project is to forecast the cash inflows and outflows necessary to support the project. This is the most crucial stage of the evaluation, and it is essential that people familiar with the organization's operations be engaged to assist in cost and income projections. The organization must consider how a better or worse economic outlook will affect the income and expenditures projected for the capital project. These conclusions will be central to making decisions about capital budgeting. In most cases, organizations should request outside assistance from an auditor, accountant, or other qualified consultant at this stage.

4. Determining the True Economic Cost of the Project

The final stage of the evaluation should include a more advanced financial analysis to determine the true economic cost of the project. The organization should implement an investment analysis technique to determine which project has the lowest net present cost and highest net present value. One of the reasons this is important is that timing differences in project-related cash flow will cause variations in true economic value. Different projects will have different cash flows at different points in time. Because of inflation, a certain sum of money received now is worth more than the same sum received later. Therefore, over time, projects that have all their costs up front end up being more costly than projects that postpone the same costs until later in the project's life cycle.

The primary method investment professionals use to assess true economic value is *discounted cash flow (DCF) analysis.* DCF analysis is the process of examining the cash flows associated with a project and discounting them at an appropriate interest rate to gain a fair measure of the true economic cost of the project. Organizations using DCF analysis should engage the services of a consultant who is familiar with this financial analysis tool to assist with the various calculations required.

D. Financing Capital Projects

The majority of organizations need some sort of outside financing to pay for capital projects. Financing can provide both benefits and risks; it is important for organizations to be fully aware of both before seeking financing.

1. Financing-Related Expenses

Obtaining the funds to finance a capital project will result in new expenses for your organization. Your organization must determine how the income will be generated to cover the additional expenses that financing entails. Organizations should, if at all possible, avoid financing major asset purchases out of existing operations. It has been proved time and time again that when capital purchases are made out of operating funds, the organization faces an increased risk of later financial difficulty. In our experience, we have found that operating funds are best earmarked exclusively for operating expenses, such as payroll, office supplies, and similar needs. Funds that are not part of the organization's operating cash flow should be designated to help finance capital items, such as equipment, buildings, or vehicles. Keeping operating funds and cash flows segregated in this manner can help organizations avoid putting undue stress on their operating budgets. The addition of a financing cost to the operations budget could put the organization at risk for failing to meet operational expenses if a cash flow problem should arise unexpectedly. Our experience confirms that this is an area of cash flow forecasting especially prone to errors. Organizations may carefully research their financing options for capital projects, but without a careful economic analysis of the necessary operating funds, cash flow problems will inevitably develop. In some cases projects fail because the cash available for operations, after paying financing expenses, is insufficient to support operational expenses.

Organizations that are evaluating financing options for capital expenditures will have to determine how large a cash outflow they can accommodate to finance the project. Capital project financial planning must take into consideration many factors, including some that are dependent on the size, structure, and financial status of the organization. For example, a small organization needing one new van to transport clients may need to lease the van instead of purchasing it, in order to conserve cash. Conversely, a larger organization may be able to buy fifty vans out of its cash reserves but need to issue $10 million in bonds to finance a new medical facility.

2. Acceptable Methods of Financing

An organization may find itself in a position where it must turn to an outside source for initial or permanent financing of a capital expenditure. Methods for securing outside capital funding include holding a capital fundraising drive, borrowing money through a mortgage, or selling bonds.

The best outside financing strategy for your organization depends on the organization's size, mission, cash flow status, and dollar needs. Frequently, organizations will need to develop separate short- and long-term plans for capital financing. For example, Universal Nonprofit obtained a mortgage for the initial financing of a new facility. However, the organization paid off the mortgage in just two years using the proceeds from a fundraising drive it conducted for this express purpose. (Universal Nonprofit was careful to negotiate a mortgage with no prepayment penalty. So even though it paid a higher interest rate, it did not have to pay a special fee for early repayment.)

Financing arrangements can be extremely complex and difficult to understand, especially for anyone who is not an expert in this field. When planning for or entering into a new financing arrangement, organizations should involve their attorneys and accountants to help explain and negotiate terms.

3. Fundraising Drives

For many organizations a capital fundraising drive can be very effective, carry low risk, and involve relatively low expenses. The simplest of capital fundraising drives will entail requesting contributions from the organization's largest donors to help fund a capital purchase. The organization may also request a commitment to give a certain amount of money over the next several years to assist in offsetting the payments from another financing source, as in the following example:

> An organization borrows $250,000 via a mortgage to make renovations to an existing facility. The largest donors to the organization state that they will provide an additional $175,000 of contributions over the next five years to assist in offsetting the cost of the renovations. The pledges receivable and the property are used as collateral for the mortgage. Thus no operating funds are used in connection with the capital project.

Organizations that are considering this form of financing may want to engage the services of a capital fundraising consultant. Generally, this type of strategy works best for organizations that have boards of directors or "friends" with substantial financial resources.

Another approach to fundraising for capital projects is seeking grants designated for this purpose. Certain foundations will grant money for capital expenditures; also, there are some limited public sources of capital funding. The state of New Jersey, for example, has issued billions of dollars in bonds over the past few years to generate money for capital-funding grants for organizations working with disabled clients.

4. Lines of Credit

Another approach to getting the funds necessary for a capital purchase of a smaller nature (such as a purchase of vehicles or office equipment) is using lines of credit. However, this could prove to be a poor decision if there is deterioration in cash flow. Sometimes, though, the advantages of using a line of credit may outweigh the disadvantages: lines of credit are typically flexible and convenient.

When seeking to use a line of credit to finance smaller capital purchases, your organization must make a decision based on its size, cash flow, the type of purchase it is making, how long a term it needs on the financing, and the amount it wants to spend. A line of credit must usually be reduced to a zero balance for at least a thirty-day period once a year. This makes the strategy impractical for permanently financing large capital costs. Lines of credit are best used as a source of cash for a limited period of time and for a relatively small capital outflow. For example, if a foundation is going to send your organization money in six months but you must make a capital purchase immediately, using a line of credit to make the capital purchase would make sense.

5. Bond Offerings

Bond offerings can be a source of substantial amounts of cash for capital needs. This option is best suited to larger organizations because setting up a bond offering is costly and complicated. Preparing bond financing will involve significant legal and professional fees. Also, the expenses associated with complying with the various legal and regulatory requirements can be high and may create a great burden on staff members. Furthermore, the ongoing legal and reporting requirements can be expensive, both in terms of fees and labor. Finally, bondholders usually require organizations to meet specific economic performance measures, to set aside specific financial reserves, and to comply with various other rules that can further complicate this financing option.

6. Bank Loans

Borrowing money was something nonprofit organizations did not do on a regular basis forty years ago. However, many nonprofits now have mortgages, lines of credit, bank loans, equipment leases, or outstanding bonds. As nonprofits have become larger and more complicated, and as their needs for cash to finance capital outlays have grown, many have turned to lenders to finance capital acquisitions.

Bank loans can be customized to fit your individual organization's needs. Organizations must review their cash flow forecasts to determine the resources available for repaying debt that is incurred through borrowing. An organization should then determine its ideal financing arrangement and identify how flexible it can be about that arrangement. The terms of the agreement should, of course, be structured to reflect the cash flow of the project being financed. For example, if a project's life is expected to be five years, the organization's finance term should not be more than five years. Your organization should also make sure to shop around for the best interest rate. This process does not have to be time consuming or labor intensive, especially when your organization can perform its research on the Internet. Organizations can use the Internet to first gather information about financing options and then fill out a single on-line application that is sent to hundreds of banks. Several Web sites currently offer this convenience. Your organization can accept the best terms offered by the lending institutions that approve its application.

7. Leases

Another method of financing and managing cash flow is through a leasing transaction. The lease can either be an *operating lease* or a *capital lease*. An operating lease requires the organization to make payments over a fixed period of time for use of the leased property or equipment. A capital lease gives the organization the option to purchase the equipment at less than market value at the end of the lease. Therefore a capital lease is really just another form of financing a capital purchase. Interest rates are often higher through a leasing transaction because there is usually a leasing agent involved. For organizations with less-than-perfect credit, leasing may be a good alternative. Organizations must scrutinize the leasing agreement just as carefully as any other financing agreement. Restrictive clauses and other stipulations that could hurt the organization's operating flexibility could be included in a leasing agreement.

Lease terms can be negotiated in the same manner as terms are negotiated for other types of financing. Leases can be a flexible and convenient source of financing if properly structured. We suggest organizations consult with an expert to assist in the negotiating and decision-making process when negotiating an unusual or complicated type of lease.

8. Aid from Public Entities

The organization may also want to consider obtaining financing through a public entity such as a local or state government. The programs operated by nonprofit organizations often alleviate some of the burden on governmental social programs, which is a good incentive for generating government support. Nonprofit organizations with programs that are highly effective and efficient may be able to convince government agencies to help finance capital projects by assisting them in the issuance of bonds.

CHAPTER 10 Cash Flow Technology

Using technology effectively is an integral part of cash flow management. When organizations improve their efficiency through making the best use of technology, they become much more productive. For example, the greatest expense category in the operating budgets and cash flow forecasts of most nonprofit organizations is employee costs. Salaries, payroll taxes, health insurance, and other fringe benefits usually consume a substantial percentage of cash outflow for nonprofits. Using technology to streamline employee functions will result in greater productivity, a reduction in employee costs, and ultimately, an improvement in cash flow. Technology also plays a major role in an area of operations outside of "back office" administrative functioning. It can also enhance client services. Organizations should explore technology that might be useful in serving clients better. Doing so will reduce operating costs as well, which will increase cash flow.

Technology is not just a tool for the for-profit sector to use in increasing the wealth of its shareholders. It can be used by nonprofits to provide greater resources to the people they serve. Recent technological advances have provided tools that can help organizations attain higher levels of operating efficiency in every aspect of operations. Computers, mobile communication devices, and other technologies can help organizations streamline the way they obtain, analyze, process, and exchange information. However, many organizations are not using these advances to their greatest benefit.

A. Technology as an Ongoing Concern

In order for organizations to maintain optimal effectiveness and efficiency, it is essential that technological improvements be considered on an ongoing basis. Management must make sincere efforts to become knowledgeable about how the latest technology can help improve operations. Furthermore, management must be willing to invest resources in upgrading technology. Optimizing the use of technology will result in substantial cash flow improvements. This can mean more cash to invest in such things as existing programs, the purchase of a capital item, or the development of a new program that helps the organization better accomplish its goals and objectives.

Technology investment should not be viewed in a short-term perspective. The initial cash outflow must be compared with the subsequent longer-term cash savings.

103

Cash flow improvements will be both direct and indirect. For example, direct savings will include wages and benefits that will no longer have to be paid when fewer personnel resources are needed to perform administrative functions. Indirect and harder-to-observe savings will result from increased accuracy in record keeping. For example, an organization may choose to convert from a manual time card system to an automated time clock, using swipe card technology. One of the results of this improvement will be an increase in the accuracy of employee time records. The real cash flow savings in this case would primarily be limited to error reduction and, in some cases, greater productivity and reduction in the cost of processing payrolls. We have observed huge variations in the costs of operating the administrative functions of organizations. We have seen a 100 percent to 500 percent difference in payroll processing costs based on how effectively an organization uses technology in payroll applications and human resources management. Similar cost savings may result in the areas of purchasing goods and paying bills.

B. Key Considerations in Technology Upgrades

Maximizing your organization's use of technology will involve several different areas of operations. One aspect of technology that cuts across all operational aspects is the reporting function. Automating reporting functions as much as possible is a major first step in maximizing technology to increase cash flow. The key technology improvement considerations addressed in the following subsections will help in automating the reporting function, as well as generally improving efficiency, effectiveness, and, ultimately, cash flow.

1. Eliminate Redundancy

First, focus on cutting all duplication of tasks to reduce the costs of producing reports. All departments and units of your organization should be using the same or highly compatible spreadsheet and word processing packages in a uniform manner. Software that accommodates all of the needs of each function of your organization is relatively easy to find, acquire, and implement. For example, most periodic reports look the same for each function and operational unit. The only differences are in the data. Therefore by setting up the report once in a common program and saving it as a template file, the organization can save time (and consequentially cash) in report preparation.

Template files, which are preformatted to direct the input of information, will create an integrated and uniform look and feel for reports. In addition, using template files will allow complete reports to be ready in a much shorter time.

Note
When a template file is opened, it should be saved under a new name to prevent changes to the original format.

Using templates to set up form letters and to preformat commonly used documents is a great time and labor saver for organizations. The preformatting approach enables organizations to distribute documents more efficiently. This leads to more current information, which leads to better decision making and, ultimately, a more professional image for the organization. Of course, saving time and money and having a more professional and competent image will help organizations increase cash flow. Contributors and funding sources want to feel confident that their funds are being used by an organization that can efficiently accomplish its goals and objectives. Organizations that project a professional image will be more likely to inspire confidence—and contributions. Many of our suggestions for reports related to cash flow forecasting lend themselves to template creation. Templates can improve the economy of cash flow operations, as your CFO or accountant can create a cash flow forecast report template, which may then be used by other staff to produce the desired report.

2. Implement an Automated Accounting System

The second office technology concern relates to implementing the appropriate type of accounting system. The most effective course of action is to implement an automated or computer-based accounting system. There are many products available on the market for different types of organizations at reasonable costs. The computer-based systems offer many advantages and are important in improving cash flow by reducing errors and staff labor. Automated postings from journals can be integrated into ledgers in seconds, which reduces human intervention (and the potential for errors) and saves time and money. Second, the computer-based systems have built-in audit functions that flag problems, such as unbalanced entries and entry errors, that otherwise could take an excessive amount of time, resources, and cash to locate and resolve. Finally, many of the computer-based accounting systems can be used to produce the reports commonly used for budgeting, monitoring, and corrective-action planning. These features further enhance cash flow by saving on the costs of report preparation and providing information in a more timely manner.

Major features organizations should look for when considering the purchase of a computer-based accounting system are:

- **Security Features.** There are several inexpensive products on the market that come with options to turn on or turn off the "audit trail." When the audit trail option is turned off, users can easily delete an entry to the financial records without creating an audit trail. However, when the audit trail feature is turned on, formal correcting journal entries must be made to change original entries. More expensive products generally come with automatic safeguards built into the software that restrict users from deleting entries.

- **Charts of Accounts.** In order for accounting software to be the most helpful to cash flow management, it must contain a powerful chart of accounts feature. This feature will allow organizations to design accounting systems capable of producing excellent detail in reports and analyses. The product should have an account number structure that allows for enough identifying data so that income and expenses can be sorted by type, source, program, location, and so on.

- **Electronic Transmission Capability.** Accounting software should have the built-in capability to exchange data electronically with other systems and with other software products. Obviously, more advanced and expensive systems will have features to make importing and exporting in different formats easier to do. There are a number of Web-based general ledger products on the market now that should be considered by organizations with the need, and adequate supporting computer systems, for them.

- **Capability to Manage Multiple Entities.** Computer-based accounting systems and software should be able to manipulate the data of several legal entities at once because many organizations will need this function.

When making purchasing decisions regarding computer accounting systems and software, organizations should seek the input of all staff who will be using the systems, the organization's auditors, and computer consultants. It is only in this way that your organization can ensure that it will purchase products that will meet all of its present and future needs.

3. Computerize Cash Flow Budgeting Processes

The third cash flow consideration is an offshoot of the second and concerns the budgeting process and cash flow forecasting. A computer-based accounting system makes it possible to analyze cash forecasts and determine when there are greater needs for cash to be on hand and when cash can be maintained in interest-bearing accounts. Furthermore, regular analyses of the timing of cash receipts and cash outflows can assist in determining where the organization stands in regard to its cash forecast. This information is essential in planning what, if any, corrective actions may need to be taken.

4. Optimize Administrative Functions

The automation of the reporting process is only half of the story when it comes to generating cash flow through technology advancements. Automating the reporting process will save a substantial number of work hours, but those productivity gains will only translate to cash flow if the productivity is properly used. Management must analyze all operations and determine which functions have become redundant or obsolete as a result of technological advances and gains in productivity (especially regarding general and administrative costs). Management must then make necessary adjustments in staffing and resource allocation to capitalize on the increases in efficiency.

While upgrading technological systems and functioning, organizations may also take the opportunity to conduct a reorganization of the office. Management and key employees should discuss and justify resource allocation to each office activity to determine if it is the best use of resources.

5. Automate Inventory Control

Inventory control is an important aspect of management for some nonprofits. Inventory can be supplies the organization uses in operations or products held for resale. Often, there is a significant investment in inventory, which should be protected with adequate controls. First, any organization that holds assets in the form of inventory (either for resale or for internal consumption) must have the appropriate software and systems in place to track and manage the inventory. For example, hospitals have large sums invested in their inventory (such as drugs, bandages, sutures, and so on). A certain portion of this inventory will ultimately be lost due to theft, breakage, or expiration. Mismanagement of inventory can result in significant expense.

For example, Universal Nonprofit runs a health care facility and maintains a large quantity of consumable supplies. Some of these supplies have expiration dates and must be used before they expire or be thrown out. In our study of the organization, we found that over $20,000 in inventory had been discarded in the prior year because it had passed its expiration date. Effective inventory technology can prevent this kind of scenario. Your organization must have a system for monitoring usage and tracking inventory effectively. Such a system will make it easier to determine the proper economic order quantity.

Inventory analysis and inventory tracking will help organizations better understand their inventory needs and operate more efficiently. The system must also include reorder limits and incorporate the *just in time* (JIT) concept to help ensure organizations order inventory at the most appropriate time. Management should periodically analyze usage to determine whether any unusual or abnormal trends are emerging that could be indicative of theft, changed demand, or product waste.

C. Cash Flow Technology and the Internet

No discussion of technology in the new millennium could ever be complete without some attention to the cash flow advantages that can be obtained by efficient use of the Internet. In fact, we believe the Internet will become a primary avenue for donors making contributions to nonprofit organizations. What this means is that organizations that do not have an Internet presence risk compromising their ability to reach donors, which can severely reduce cash flow. An example of the potential impact of Internet donations could be observed during the 2000 presidential primaries. A single victory in one state yielded millions of dollars in campaign donations over the Internet in less than seven days for one candidate. This should convince nonprofit organizations to design their Web sites to accept donations.

It is highly desirable for organizations to develop Web pages that convey their missions and provide donors with news and notices of special events. Organizations must also devote resources to promoting their Web sites so that potential donors will be directed to them. One important way of doing this is to make sure people can find your Web site when conducting searches using the major search engines. (See Chapter Thirteen for a lengthier discussion of using the Internet to enhance cash flow.)

1. Internet Commerce

Using the capabilities of Internet commerce can be a great way of enhancing cash flow. In order to do this, organizations must have a way of accepting credit card payments via the Internet, either directly on their sites or through another site. There are Web sites set up for the express purpose of providing information to donors about various nonprofit organizations. Some of these sites have started to accept donations on-line, which are then forwarded to the nonprofits registered with the Web site.

Organizations should also consider Internet joint ventures with other nonprofits in the same line of service. These joint ventures have the advantage of lower start-up costs and the ability to draw contributors who would not otherwise be part of the organization's donor pool. For example, a joint Web site with another nonprofit or group of organizations will bring your organization to the attention of donors who are already involved with nonprofits in the same service segment. A joint venture with for-profit Web sites can potentially draw a completely new set of contributors to nonprofits in your organization's service segment.

2. On-Line Bill Payment

The ability to pay bills on-line is another cash flow management tool available to organizations that use the Internet. This service allows organizations to remit payment to vendors exactly at the moment that they are due, as the funds are almost instantaneously transferred to the vendors' accounts. On-line bill payment with vendors who also use this service allows the organization to take a JIT approach to managing cash disbursements. Using this technology will lead to greater cash flow for several reasons. First, labor is saved in that checks do not have to be written, recorded, signed, and mailed. In addition, there are no postal charges. Perhaps the greatest boon to cash flow is that funds can be maintained in interest-bearing accounts right up until the moment they must be transferred to the vendor.

On-line banking does not only benefit the organization through direct cash flow improvement; it also offers advantages in the areas of information management, monitoring, and recording. Using on-line banking to its fullest capacity will allow management to monitor cash positions closely and with minimal resource expenditure. For example, organizations can determine with a few mouse clicks exactly when an electronic funds transfer has been received. A few more mouse clicks will allow organizations to move idle funds into interest-bearing accounts, such as savings and money market accounts, so that income can be earned on the funds until they are needed.

Organizations may derive some of the same benefits without using on-line banking by paying certain vendors, such as landlords and utilities, via automatic payment options established by the vendor. However, organizations should only opt for this service when they have an ongoing relationship with a vendor who has proved trustworthy. Recovery of fraudulent or erroneous charges can be difficult and time consuming. We recently consulted with a client who had been the victim of automated-payment overcharging by a vendor who was having financial difficulties. Fortunately, the charges were caught early enough to be questioned and recovered.

3. Program Enhancements via the Internet

We believe our example of the effectiveness of the Internet in helping political candidates raise money is just the proverbial "tip of the iceberg." Expanding your organization's use of the Internet can radically change your operations and enhance your efficiency and effectiveness. Obviously, using the Internet creatively is an expansive topic and beyond the scope of this book. However, we do believe the Internet is a resource for improving cash flow. Thus we have included many relevant suggestions concerning this issue. For example, communication speed can become a cash flow concern, and it is enhanced when organizations use the Internet. No other communication device (phone, fax, or mail) gives you the ability to so actively communicate on a real-time basis the amount of information that can be communicated via the Internet. Organizations may use e-mail to send out important information to clients and provide hyperlinks to sites that might be useful to them. The full potential of the Internet to help your organization improve its cash flow and be a much better service provider has yet to be achieved. We suggest you think carefully about how the Internet can revolutionize your services.

D. Additional Considerations for Using Technology to Improve Cash Flow

There are many other specific ways to generate cash flow and decrease expenses that individual managers and employees can exploit. One relatively simple one that has been used successfully by almost every type of organization and business that sells inventory is to implement a toll-free number for customers to use in ordering products.

Otherwise, improving cash flow in this area of nonprofit operations is the same as it is in most others: only spend what must be spent, hold on to cash as long as possible, and make your assets generate as much cash as possible.

In conclusion, we strongly suggest that organizations thoroughly research every technology upgrade before it is planned, to ensure that it is genuinely necessary and supported by economic evidence that it will improve productivity. A single technology upgrade will never be enough to change an organization. It is necessary to change the culture and to reward employees and line managers who exhibit innovative thought in regard to increasing productivity. Incentive programs can create a more innovative culture among employees. Offering employees a nominal percentage of the savings a productivity improvement idea generates will likely inspire some worthwhile ideas. Quarterly brainstorming sessions with an open-minded atmosphere will also encourage a more creative and dynamic culture.

Regardless of the methods used to involve employees in technology and productivity improvement, we cannot overemphasize the importance of listening to the very people who will use the technology the most. Often, there are practical considerations even the most keen observers will miss without ongoing input from those involved in the relevant processes and functions. Getting the input of the primary users of the technology before it is implemented will increase the chances that they will be supportive once it is up and running.

PART THREE

Specific Cash Flow Management Strategies for Various Types of Income

ONE OF THE MAJOR PRINCIPLES on which *The Cash Flow Management Book for Nonprofits* is based is that the strategies organizations must use to manage cash flow effectively will vary depending on the types of income they receive. In this section we provide specific information on cash flow management and planning for many types of nonprofit income. The different types of income are grouped into separate chapters so that organizations can easily locate and review the ones applicable to them.

Each chapter covers the major issues and unique cash flow implications for the featured category of income. Some of the broader topics we address are:

- Cash flow forecasting and planning

- Cash flow reporting, monitoring, and analysis

- Applicable technology issues

- Cash flow problems and solutions

CHAPTER 11 Program Service Income

According to IRS statistics, charging fees for performing services is the largest source of income for nonprofits. Examples of organizations that derive substantial income from this source include schools and universities, health care–related agencies, and mental health clinics. Organizations for which the primary source of income is program service revenue face most of the same challenges that for-profit businesses do. In order to run efficiently, there must be well-designed systems of policies and procedures in place to carry out financial operations. Proper controls are also necessary to ensure that the policies and procedures are consistently applied. Some of the major cash flow issues, obstacles, and strategies applicable to program service income are summarized in Exhibits 11.1 and 11.2.

A. Effective Policies and Procedures

Designing effective systems to optimize cash flow will require starting "at the beginning." In other words, organizations should evaluate their policies and procedures starting from the initial contact with the client. Often this first contact (registration, in many cases) is the most important interaction with a client because it is the best opportunity for information gathering. And having the correct information is often necessary for billing, collection, and compliance with external regulations. Ensuring data integrity—that is, ensuring all collected and posted data are complete and accurate—is an essential consideration at this point in the process. Later on, data integrity can be very hard to maintain, especially when initial efforts have been ineffective or misdirected. It is a good idea to inform clients or patients before initial registration of the exact data or documents that will be needed. The pre-registration process ideally should be performed by staff specifically trained in interviewing. This will reduce anxiety for the client and will promote more efficient and accurate data collection and registration. Policies and procedures related to the initial contact with the client should provide the organization with at least the following information:

- Client's full name, address, phone number, and other necessary identifying numbers (such as Social Security number, insurance group number, or case number)

EXHIBIT 11.1   **Program Service Income: Key Cash Flow Issues and Common Pitfalls**

KEY ISSUES

- Fee-for-service nonprofits earn income through the rendering of services, as do businesses.
- Cash flow is dependent on efficient and timely billing and collection procedures.
- Maintaining positive cash flow involves keeping expenses per client served as low as possible.
- Cash flow in organizations that rely on program service income is often heavily dependent on third-party reimbursement (such as from insurance companies and federal, state, and local government).

COMMON PITFALLS

- Failing to bill for all services rendered or for all clients served.
- Failing to get proper payer information, resulting in late payment or nonpayment of bills.
- Failing to use correct billing classifications, resulting in refusal to pay for services.
- Failing to issue bills promptly.
- Failing to properly follow up on collections in accounts receivable.
- Failing to use staff and facilities in the most efficient manner.
- Failing to properly project expenses or having high expenses per client contact.
- Failing to have in place adequate billing trigger mechanisms at points of service that start the bill-generation process.
- Failing to obtain required written authorization for services rendered (as is necessary in some managed-care environments).
- Failing to collect copayments at the time of service.

- Payer's name, fax number, and contact person (when the client is not the payer)
- Any required authorizations needed on initial contact or on an ongoing basis
- Any required documentation
- Reimbursement rate or payment method
- Relevant time frames for billing and collection applicable to initial contact and ongoing service

B. Cash Flow Forecasting and Planning

As already mentioned, projecting and planning cash flow and creating cash flow forecasts in fee-for-service organizations will be similar to conducting these activities in for-profit service-related businesses. Billing and collection efficiency and success will

---

EXHIBIT 11.2   **Program Service Income: Cash Flow Problems and Solutions**

PROBLEM

1. High rate of uncollected bills leading to high bad debt expense.

SOLUTION

1. Review billing and collection procedures, taking the following steps:

   a. Review pre-registration procedures to ensure patient or client is aware of information necessary for registration.

   b. Review registration procedures to ensure that all necessary information is obtained, recorded, and substantiated.

   c. Review systems in place for prompt billing, regular late-payment reminders, and fulfillment of requests for additional information or actions by third-party payers.

   d. Review systems in place for complying with documentation requirements and regulations.

   e. Encourage payment at the point of service to the extent possible.

   f. Consider engaging the services of a professional collection agency.

---

have the greatest impact on cash flow. Thus the most important factor in cash flow forecasting and planning will be developing and using effective procedures and policies related to the registration process.

In terms of projecting income and generating cash flow forecasts, organizations will most often use formulas that are based on likelihood of receiving cash. Also, modifying the prior period's financial data for changes that might occur in income or expenses is an essential step in cash flow forecasting and planning. Following are some of the types of data that will be helpful in these endeavors:

- Services billed in the prior year, quarter, or month
- Revenues collected in the prior year, quarter, or month
- Amount and timing of expenses in the prior year
- Use of facilities, staff, and time (such as number of rooms, staff, time, and so on, available for services versus percentage of use)
- Anticipated changes in client or customer use (such as expected increases or decreases in client contacts)
- Anticipated changes in reimbursement rates and timing
- Anticipated changes in program expenses

C. Cash Flow Reporting, Monitoring, and Analysis

Organizations that conduct fee-for-service activities must have in place comprehensive financial management systems that link many departments and functions. This is the most important aspect in ensuring that all relevant financial operations are incorporated in cash flow reporting, monitoring, and analysis. Organizations must review procedures for documenting all billing, collection, purchasing, payroll, and other expense information and for making sure this information is substantiated. Moreover, once this information is obtained, it must be communicated in understandable formats.

Cash flow forecasting for program service income will require the input of every department involved in either generating income or incurring expenses. The finance department will use information obtained from these sources to develop cash flow forecasts for reporting, monitoring, and analysis. How often and to what extent this is done will depend on the size, complexity, and needs of the organization.

D. Cash Flow Technology Issues

Program service income is probably one of the most information-dependent income streams. Client records, registration information, client contact or service provision records, and billing and collection data must all become part of the organization's databanks. Moreover, the information must be updated and integrated on an ongoing basis. Effective computer hardware and software are essential to maintaining good records. Organizations will have to evaluate their unique needs to determine which hardware and software products will be of most benefit to them. Programs for managing information, generating bills, and so on, should have the capacity to link departments and functions. In addition, there are many software companies that offer programs for managing information in particular types of organizations, such as health care or mental health organizations. These systems should be evaluated for practicality before your organization decides to purchase them. For example, in order for a system to be useful, many organizations will need to have the ability to accept credit card payments from clients or patients and electronic payments from insurers and other payers.

E. Additional Considerations

As stated previously, the most important considerations in maintaining good cash flow in organizations that depend on program service income are:

- Obtaining proper information
- Ensuring that policies and procedures are in place to record and make this information available to relevant departments and personnel
- Developing and implementing policies and procedures to ensure prompt follow-through

Another aspect of operations to consider in improving cash flow for program service income is making optimal use of staff and facilities. For example, if the organization has ten offices in which services are performed and fifteen staff members who perform the services, the organization should have the rooms in use by clients the majority of the time or should consider making other income-producing use of the rooms or staff. In a broader context organizations should examine the profitability of each of their program services. To the extent that it is compatible with the organization's mission, the focus on less profitable services should be minimized, and the focus on more profitable ones should be maximized.

CHAPTER 12

Income from Sales of Inventory

Although few types of nonprofit organizations sell inventory as their primary source of income, many organizations supplement their overall cash flow in this manner. Examples of nonprofits for which sales of inventory are the largest percentage of income are gift shops and mail order book-selling operations run by professional organizations. Many nonprofits generate supplemental income through sales of promotional items such as T-shirts and other accessories that feature the organization's logo.

Some of the major cash flow issues, obstacles, and strategies applicable to income from sales of inventory are summarized in Exhibits 12.1 and 12.2.

EXHIBIT 12.1   **Sales of Inventory: Key Cash Flow Issues and Common Pitfalls**

KEY ISSUES

- Establishing effective purchasing strategies—goods being sold must be obtained at the best possible price.

- Locating good suppliers—use vendors that deliver the inventory on time, in good condition, and that provide responsive service.

- Maintaining low inventory—keep the amount of money invested in inventory low by arranging for suppliers to deliver orders to customers promptly.

- Optimizing ordering-versus-holding costs through economic ordering quantities or a similar inventory optimization method designed to reduce the costs associated with maintaining a large inventory.

COMMON PITFALLS

- Paying too much for products, services, or overhead, which reduces the profitability of sales.

- Billing or collecting for purchased products too slowly.

- Failing to budget for UBIT payments for sales of items subject to UBIT.

- Maintaining a large inventory and incurring the associated costs of obsolescence, insurance, storage, carrying, theft, and so on.

- Failing to collect sales tax when applicable (note that state sales tax laws vary in this area).

EXHIBIT 12.2	Sales of Inventory: Cash Flow Problems and Solutions

PROBLEMS

1. The dollar value of current inventory equals one year's revenue.

2. The accounting department's analysis reveals that your organization is not making a profit selling products.

SOLUTIONS

1. Set up a more effective ordering system. If there is this much inventory on hand, your organization is probably ordering too much inventory or not selling enough products. Organizations should not start selling products without adequate market research. Unless proper inventory turnover can be achieved, an organization with this problem will experience severe cash flow problems.

2. Examine the price your organization is paying for products versus the sales price. Is there enough of a profit margin, when selling and administrative costs are factored in, to make a profit on each unit sold? The other possibility is that products are leaving your organization's premises without being paid for. Some products are easily misplaced or stolen. Organizations must maintain adequate inventory control to prevent theft and earn profits from sales activities.

A. Effective Policies and Procedures

Organizations that participate in any activity involving sales of inventory and that would like to improve cash flow related to this activity should begin by reviewing relevant policies and procedures. Cash flow from sales of inventory will be most dependent on having in place and following policies and procedures to perform effective purchasing, billing, collections, order fulfillment, and inventory management.

B. Cash Flow Forecasting and Planning

Cash flow forecasting and planning related to sales of inventory will require organizations to review the following variables on a regular basis:

- Expenses associated with selling the inventory
- Time frames in which these expenses must be paid
- Sales volume that will be necessary to create a "profit"
- Likelihood that this volume will be achieved
- Proper allocation of administrative costs (overhead) to identify real "profits" on each item sold

Other issues that should be considered in cash flow forecasting and planning for sales of inventory are prior years' sales of inventory, prior years' expenses, anticipated seasonal fluctuations in sales, anticipated price increases for production or fulfillment (including shipping and handling charges, advertising, wholesale cost of the items, and so on), the "perishability" of the items (if they are likely to go out of style or otherwise decrease in value), and any changes in expenses related to employees who will be responsible for managing the program.

C. Cash Flow Reporting, Monitoring, and Analysis

Cash flow reporting for sales of inventory will be more straightforward than it is for other types of income generation. Accounting and reporting will require an efficient system of data communication between all departments and the accounting and finance department. Those involved in the ongoing administration of the program and day-to-day operations must understand the importance of accuracy and completeness when submitting records to the finance department. At minimum, the accounting and finance department should have all necessary information readily available to produce monthly reports on merchandise sold, cash received, and the number and amount of accounts receivable. Expense data that will be beneficial to have readily accessible on an ongoing basis include:

- Data on bad debts (accounts receivable never collected). A high bad debt expense indicates a review of the policy used to authorize credit extension to clients is necessary.
- Data on costs related to obtaining the inventory.
- Data on employee compensation related to sales.
- Data on order fulfillment, shipping, and other associated expenses.
- Data on advertising expenses.

Ideally, the accounting department should be able to generate comprehensive monthly reports that include detailed and accurate income and expense information for this revenue stream.

Organizations that depend on sales of inventory for income should be performing several special financial analyses related to these operations. In Chapter Eight we discussed the importance of computing and understanding working capital. Organizations for which inventory makes up a large amount of assets or generates a large amount of income (for example, greater than 15 percent of revenue) should be performing the analyses outlined in Exhibit 12.3.

D. Cash Flow Technology Issues

Obviously, cash flow technology for sales of inventory will involve having adequate computer systems in place to track orders, stock, payments, shipping details, returns, and other types of ordering and fulfillment processing. Depending on the size of the

EXHIBIT 12.3	Financial Analyses for Organizations with Substantial Inventory-Based Assets or Income

- Quick ratio: the sum of cash, cash equivalents, and net receivables, divided by current liabilities. Unlike the working capital calculation described in Chapter Eight, the quick ratio does not include inventory, or items identified as prepaid expenses, in current assets. This is a more conservative analysis of liquidity that will be more useful than other liquidity analyses for organizations substantially involved in selling inventory. In the quick ratio liquidity is generally adequate if cash, cash equivalents, and net receivables exceed current liabilities. The stronger the quick ratio (that is, the greater the amount by which cash, cash equivalents, and net receivables exceed current liabilities), the better your organization's financial strength and cash flow.

- Ratio of inventory to working capital: the value of the organization's inventory expressed as a percentage of the organization's working capital. When inventory is a large percentage of total working capital, it may be an indicator of future (or present) cash flow problems.

- Accounts receivable turnover: the organization's credit sales divided by the average accounts receivable. This computation will indicate how long it takes for an organization to turn its credit sales into cash. Obviously, the longer it takes, the more damaging it is to cash flow.

- Inventory turnover: the cost of goods sold divided by the average inventory. This computation will indicate how quickly an organization "turns over" its inventory. A quick turnover is good for cash flow. A slow turnover may indicate that inventory levels are too high.*

Note: This is in no way an exhaustive list of the calculations and accounting procedures used to monitor inventory operations. However, we believe these are the most important and relevant for the majority of nonprofits that sell inventory.

*"Slow" and "quick" are relative terms. Low-priced inventory items typically turn over faster than expensive ones. Consult with your accountant to determine the turnover ratio your organization should be trying to achieve.

organization, the volume and variety of products sold, the order fulfillment arrangements, and so on, the most practical computer systems may be very simple or quite complex. A number of specialized sales registers linked to computer systems are available for control of sales, cash receipts, and inventory control. In addition, bar-coding capabilities, for use at the cash register and for inventory control, should be part of any inventory computer system. Regardless of the size or complexity of sales operations and the computer hardware available, it is important for organizations to have adequate software installed. A number of excellent software packages exist that will provide a comprehensive platform for tracking, reporting, and analyzing sales data. Nonprofits should always get the recommendations of their accountants or appropriate consultants when upgrading or investing in new technology. As discussed in Chapter Ten, cash flow technology for sales of inventory will ideally include use of the Internet for sales, customer service, and so on.

E. Additional Considerations

1. Theft

Whenever there is inventory available for sale, unfortunately, it is also available for theft. Some studies have shown that theft by employees is even more common than theft by customers. Organizations that maintain stock, whether on-site or in a warehouse, must have controls in place to make sure they are not losing money through pilferage of inventory. Regular inventory checks are essential in avoiding stock loss due to theft. Inventory should be checked when stock is received from vendors, at regular intervals while it is stored, and before stock supply is replenished.

2. Deterioration

Any time inventory is held for more than a modest period, there is the risk of a loss in value from physical deterioration. Organizations that maintain inventory must consider this factor in cash flow management, especially regarding income and expense projection and planning.

3. Fulfillment Options

Organizations that sell inventory should consider the option of outsourcing all fulfillment-related tasks. Contracting with a fulfillment house will relieve the organization of many time-consuming and potentially expensive functions, such as shipping, maintaining, storing, and checking inventory. Moreover, this option often turns out to be less expensive than if the organization conducted these activities itself.

4. Use of Volunteers and UBIT

Organizations that use volunteers in conducting their inventory sales may avoid having to pay UBIT. This is the case in many thrift shops operated by nonprofit organizations. However, in order to take advantage of this rule, volunteer labor must account for 85 percent of total labor. Otherwise, UBIT may be applicable for income generated through sales of inventory. In order for a tax-exempt organization to be exempt from paying this tax, the organization must be able to prove that the activity (in this case, sales of inventory) is substantially related to the organization's tax-exempt purpose or that the activity falls under one or more IRS exclusion codes. Consult your auditor if this issue might be applicable to your organization. (See Chapter Eight for a more detailed discussion of UBIT.)

CHAPTER 13 Income from Contributions

There are many tax-exempt organizations that depend entirely or almost entirely on contributions for support. Included among these would be the majority of foundations and almost all churches and religious organizations, which are supported primarily by contributions. There are also other types of organizations that would be considered contributor funded, even though they do not rely on actual cash contributions from donors. For example, organizations that hold contributions for disbursement to other nonprofits would count contributions as their primary or sole revenue stream. Some of the major cash flow issues, obstacles, and strategies applicable to income from contributions are summarized in Exhibits 13.1 and 13.2.

EXHIBIT 13.1   Contributions: Key Cash Flow Issues and Common Pitfalls

KEY ISSUES

- Developing effective and cost-efficient solicitation methods.

- Making the contribution process easy for contributors.

- Creating systems to process contributions and provide the quickest access to the funds.

- Establishing controls to safeguard contributions from theft.

- Creating and implementing income projection methodologies that are appropriate for contributions.

COMMON PITFALLS

- Projecting future income inaccurately.

- Failing to deposit funds in a timely manner.

- Allowing a poor internal control environment, resulting in theft of contributions.

- Using inadequate collection methods, resulting in failure to collect promised contributions.

- Using ineffective fundraising strategies, resulting in high expenses without satisfactory donations.

- Failing to "prequalify" donors in pledge situations, resulting in some pledges not being honored.

EXHIBIT 13.2   **Contributions: Cash Flow Problems and Solutions**

PROBLEMS

1. Low ratio of pledged contributions to collected contributions.

2. High ratio of fundraising expenses to fundraising income.

3. Low rate of repeat donations.

SOLUTIONS

1. Develop and implement a follow-up system with reminders to those who pledge donations. Restate how their donations will help your organization, and offer them easy payment options.

2. Review fundraising expenses, especially those involving direct mail or service contracts with fundraising companies or individuals. Comparison-shop to determine if your organization is paying a reasonable and competitive price for the services. Review solicitation techniques for effectiveness. Implement new strategies to increase your organization's rate of return.

3. Make sure that systems are in place for prompt and appropriate acknowledgment of donations and that requests for additional donations accompany or follow such acknowledgments.

Improving cash flow management for organizations that depend on donors for support will require an analysis focusing on the following three basic questions:

1. How are contributions solicited?

2. How are contributions made?

3. How is income from contributions projected and budgeted?

When organizations have good systems in place with regard to these three areas of operation, cash flow will be optimal. However, there are many aspects to each of these issues that must be addressed to produce effective cash flow. The latter two questions that should be asked when analyzing cash flow management in contributor-funded organizations will be covered in later sections on cash flow forecasting, accounting, and technology. The first question, regarding solicitation of contributions, is probably the most important aspect of ensuring good cash flow in donor-funded organizations. The relative success or failure of solicitation methods will determine the quantity and timing of receipt of the income. Soliciting contributions creates most of the expenses associated with this type of funding, thereby greatly affecting the cost side of the cash flow equation.

Thus organizations that are contributor funded have one cash flow concern that supersedes all others: the consistency of their receipt of cash. This is due to the fact that—unlike some other income streams—it is almost impossible to accurately predict (and sometimes even to understand) fluctuations in income from contributions during a fiscal year. Improving cash flow in contributor-funded organizations will predominantly involve making this source of income as consistent as possible.

Note

Although the advice in this chapter holds true for almost every area of cash flow improvement, we believe it is especially true for cash flow improvement in contributor-funded organizations. Organizations that are considering implementation of any new cash flow enhancement activity should consult with the appropriate experienced experts, or skilled and experienced board members, and with staff or outside legal and finance professionals. Many of the strategies for improving cash flow that we describe in this chapter can be very complicated, and conducting them incorrectly may result in considerable damage to an organization. If your nonprofit plans a new direct-mail campaign, consult the appropriate fundraising professional, relevant board members, and members of your legal and finance staff. If your organization is planning to launch a Web site, Web design and administration consultants are invaluable in making it a worthwhile and profitable addition to your organization's resources. If your organization is forgoing consultants because it lacks the resources to hire them, keep in mind how much it might cost if the new activity turns out to be unsuccessful. Then reconsider other options for cutting expenses and find a good consultant.

A. Effective Methods for Soliciting Contributions

One of the best ways of increasing the consistency of contributions is to create mechanisms to keep donors aware of the organization and what it is doing. The saying "out of sight, out of mind" may have its greatest applicability in situations where you are trying to get people to part with their money. Organizations that can stay on the minds of their regular contributors will probably receive contributions of a greater amount and with greater frequency. One strategy for keeping your organization at the forefront of your potential contributors' thought is to publish an inexpensive quarterly newsletter. Other strategies involve direct-mail campaigns, telemarketing, and other traditional methods of appealing to potential contributors. One of the most effective strategies for improving contribution revenue is to "land the big one"—to get one very large donor that will help fund solicitation efforts and will inspire other donors to give more than they would have otherwise.

1. Strategies for Effective Fundraising Newsletters

Publishing a newsletter is a relatively simple idea and is often treated as an "afterthought" by many organizations. Nonetheless, offering a newsletter as a product and a service has proven to be a wonderful way for organizations to make money while promoting their missions. The following subsections discuss some of the most effective ways to use newsletters.

a. Include the Latest News Pertaining to Your Organization. A newsletter should include a section with updates on the organization's activities. Relevant items for this section would be any successes the organization has enjoyed, new projects or programs in the works (especially those that might need support through donations), any appointments or changes to the organization's leadership, and any media activity related to the organization.

b. Include Something Useful to the Contributor. People will be more likely to read the newsletter if it includes something interesting and relevant to them personally. Any such articles should also be related to the organization's mission or programs. For example, an organization that runs programs for improving the health of inner-city youth might feature an article on recent advances in the treatment of asthma. An organization dedicated to providing services for the chronically mentally ill might contain an article on depression or anxiety. An organization that offers legal assistance to immigrants might include a piece on immigration law.

c. Thank Contributors. Including a regular listing of contributors at different levels of support is a good way to express gratitude publicly for supporters' generosity. Assigning various titles based on the amount of contributions, such as "benefactor," "supporter," "helper," and so on, is a nice way to acknowledge people and businesses that have donated funds to your organization.

d. Make the Newsletter a Product. It is easier to get people to make a contribution if they believe they are receiving something of value for their money. If your organization can put together a newsletter that is interesting and informative enough for people to "subscribe," this is an excellent strategy for getting a consistent annual or semiannual donation. For example, a newsletter of an arts institution that is published quarterly and contains program-related and other relevant news, a calendar of events, an article about the arts or an artist, a listing of contributors, and a solicitation for funds for a specific project could be "subscribed to" for $60 annually.

e. Use the Newsletter to Generate Sales for Other Products. Including in your newsletter a listing, order form, toll-free number, fax number, e-mail address, and payment information for products your organization sells is a great way of linking fundraising efforts and reducing overhead expenses. For example, your organization could reserve a section of the newsletter for photos or illustrations of promotional items the organization is selling, descriptions of special events to which the organization is selling tickets, and so on.

2. Elements of Effective Direct-Mail Campaigns

a. Timing. Everyone with a mailbox knows that during certain times of the year solicitations from charities will arrive with greater frequency. This is not a coincidence. Giving patterns have shown that people are more likely to make donations in the period just before Thanksgiving and around the beginning of the year (especially in colder climates). Likewise, there are definitely times of the year when people are quite unlikely to give, such as during the middle of the summer when they are on vacation. People are also more likely to make contributions when the campaign takes place on the anniversary of a historical or other special event or when the campaign is an annual undertaking.

Timing is so important in the overall success of a direct-mail campaign that missing the target date by as little as two weeks can result in a failed campaign. Poorly timed direct-mail pieces might be ignored by their intended audience, causing a rate of return so low that it might not even pay for the campaign. This is why it is essential that organizations choose a mailing house that is efficient and professional, with a proven track record of prompt service. Another concern in direct-mail solicitation is the accuracy of the mailing list. Organizations should make sure that they provide correct names, addresses, and other contact information and that the mailing house uses this information properly. Accuracy is also a concern when purchasing mailing lists from list brokers or other organizations. Review lists for accuracy and completeness before forwarding mailing information to a mailing house or including the information in in-house mailing lists.

Note
Whenever direct-mail pieces are returned and marked "addressee unknown," organizations should make sure to update databases and mailing lists to reflect this circumstance. Such attention to detail will end up saving organizations a lot of money in the long run.

b. Audience. Organizations must decide to whom they want to appeal with a direct-mail campaign and how to identify and reach such individuals. Effectively pinpointing groups of likely donors will ensure a higher rate of return and greater cost efficiency. Conversely, unfocused campaigns or those that are based on invalid demographic information or assumptions might end up wasting a lot of time and money. In fact, failure to properly focus a direct-mail campaign may result in serious economic consequences for organizations. Obviously, some of the best sources of likely donors are mailing lists from the organization's prior fundraising drives. Other mailing lists of individuals who have given to similar causes or who are professionally, personally, or otherwise involved with the organization's mission may be purchased. Buying appropriate mailing lists will often be a most effective use for money in your fundraising budget.

c. Contents. The contents of a direct-mail solicitation will be pivotal in enticing people to donate. Enclosures should represent your organization and its cause in a manner that is congruent with the organization's mission. For example, if your organization is a community-based agency, direct mail should not be on linen paper with gold-embossed lettering and four-color photographs. Expensive-looking or ostentatious mail pieces might send an unintended message about your organization's priorities. Other things that make a negative impression include anything written poorly, in jargon, or in a difficult style, anything too long or in any way excessive, anything containing unjustifiable immodesty, and anything that is overly cluttered with graphics or information.

As is the case when preparing a newsletter, keep in mind that potential donors will be more likely to give if they feel they are getting something from the mailing other than a request for money. Including a well-prepared newsletter with the direct-mail piece is one way of achieving this. If the organization does not produce a newsletter, consider including several pages describing organization news and events. Perhaps the most important enclosure in a direct-mail campaign is a statement describing precisely what the funds will be used to accomplish. If feasible, include quantifiable measures. For example, an organization that feeds and clothes the homeless might include the following statement:

> Supporters ($50 donation) will provide a hot meal to fifteen homeless people.
>
> Affiliates ($200 donation) will provide a warm winter coat for ten homeless people this winter.
>
> Patrons ($500 donation) will provide seven homeless people who are interviewing for jobs with professional attire.
>
> Golden Circle Donors ($5,000 donation) will equip a mobile unit to provide meals for the homeless in our mobile outreach area.

Depending on the organization or project being funded, it might not be possible to provide this type of information. However, when possible, offering some tangible picture of where donations are going will increase donor generosity and confidence.

d. Acknowledgment. Providing quick written acknowledgment is an indispensable step in laying the groundwork for future donations. The acknowledgment should include a statement of gratitude, a statement of how the donation will be used (quantifiably if possible), a statement of the tax deductibility of the donation, and perhaps another solicitation.

e. Cost Efficiency. Direct-mail campaigns can be notoriously expensive, especially when the majority of the work is outsourced to firms specializing in this service. Organizations must make sure they shop around and avoid contracting with a direct-mail firm whose fees consume an unreasonable percentage of overall donations. There are many such firms in existence—some that charge fees so exorbitant that they could only be categorized as scams preying on inexperienced nonprofits.

When interviewing fundraising consultants or firms that will be providing fundraising services, organizations should ask about the "expected rate of return or response," based on the fundraiser's experience with similar organizations. Although this information is not the only important consideration, it will provide an idea of the consultant's or firm's criteria for success, which may be used later for comparative purposes.

3. Special Considerations for Telemarketing Campaigns

Telemarketing seems to be an area that has attracted some businesses that would rather take high profits than act ethically. Nonprofits that are interested in enlisting the services of telemarketing firms need to be aware that some firms charge very high fees. In some cases, after fees are subtracted, organizations end up receiving only a very small portion of each donation. For example, some telemarketing firms take up to 75 percent of donation revenue as their compensation. A recent news article identified a telemarketing firm receiving over 90 percent of the revenues it generated. This has become such a widespread problem that we suggest that organizations only enter into contracts with telemarketing firms that charge a flat fee for their services.

In addition, for organizations that want to save money on telemarketing, we suggest using experts to design a telemarketing approach but using volunteers to conduct the actual campaign.

Note

Our cautions are not intended to condemn the entire telemarketing services industry. Organizations that are interested in using such services should conduct thorough research into the companies they are considering and obtain references.

B. Cash Flow Forecasting and Planning

As stated previously, income from contributions is probably the hardest type of income to project accurately. Thus cash flow planning and budgeting will involve a greater amount of preparation and a greater amount of uncertainty.

With regard to income projection, organizations must make sure that they are using the most accurate projection methodology. When developing or choosing income projection methodology, organizations will have to consider such variables as the following:

- The type of contributions and the form in which they are received
- Any seasonal or yearly donation patterns
- Outside variables that might affect the timing or quantity of donations
- The nature of the organization and its services
- Characteristics of donors

There are statistics often used by direct-mail firms to identify desirable or expected rates of return for direct-mail campaigns. However, these may be arbitrary and not applicable in many situations. A more relevant number for organizations projecting income from contributions is the historical rate of return for the campaign or for the group of donors. Organizations that have been fundraising for a number of years and have built up a donor base will be able to use demographic and other information about giving patterns to make more accurate projections.

When launching a new campaign or reaching out to a new donor pool, organizations must create budgets to reflect the uncertainty of this income. For example, anticipated funds from a first-time contribution campaign should never be budgeted for essential services or general operations. If such a campaign were to fail, the organization's survival could be at risk. A far more prudent idea would be to budget these moneys for opportunities to enhance operations or as seed money for other endeavors.

The income side of cash flow forecasting, planning, and budgeting can be very uncertain. Therefore it is important for contributor-funded organizations to do everything in their power to make sure the expense side of the budget is accurate. Organizations must make sure their projections of fundraising expenses are realistic. Contacting and obtaining estimates from those with whom the organization will be contracting for services is essential. These might include consultants, mail houses, or direct-mail and telemarketing firms.

Another concept for effective cash flow forecasting in contributor-funded organizations is to develop individual budgets for each project or activity for which there is fundraising. The budget should contain a description of the project's goals and how much income from contributions will be needed—and by what date—to accomplish each goal. Assembling such detailed expense information will help in cash flow planning and will allow the organization to supply prospective donors with detailed information on how their contributions will be used.

C. Cash Flow Reporting, Monitoring, and Analysis

Accounting for income from contributions will vary in its complexity based on the characteristics of the contributions themselves. When all income received is in the form of cash (or checks, direct deposits, or credit cards payments), accounting will be straightforward and based on the actual value of the contribution. However, when contributions are in other forms, accounting for them can become complicated. For example, when a contribution is made through a nonprofit that accepts contributions for later distribution to other nonprofits, the accounting for these transactions will have to incorporate all applicable rules.

Noncash contributions, such as contributions of stock, real estate, or other items of value, will require organizations to perform specialized accounting steps. For example, organizations might have to find or develop appropriate methodologies to appropriately value noncash contributions for accounting purposes.

Cash flow reporting, monitoring, and analysis are very important for organizations that depend on income from contributions. Using appropriate monitoring and analysis is the only way organizations will be able to improve the accuracy of future cash flow projections. Effective accounting and monitoring will also reduce the chances of theft or fraud.

D. Cash Flow Technology Issues

The manner in which contributions are donated, processed, deposited, and recorded are major cash flow technology considerations. Organizations must use the technology available to them to create a system that makes it as easy, safe, and efficient as possible for the donor to contribute. The system must then allow for these contributions to be properly recorded and all relevant data to be captured and entered into the organization's systems. Procedures to ensure internal control should be part of this technology, as should mechanisms for analyzing contribution data.

An important aspect of technology for contributor-funded organizations is having efficient systems in place to provide access to contributed funds in a timely manner. Collecting the donation, recording it, depositing it in the bank, and acknowledging receipt of the donation are top priorities. The following subsections contain suggestions for using technology to improve cash flow from contributions.

1. Electronic Funds Transfer

Using electronic funds transfer (EFT) to receive contributions from donors can significantly increase the frequency and predictability of cash receipts. EFT operates in a similar manner to direct deposit and other automatic credit and debit programs. An agreed-on sum is transferred directly from the donor's bank account (or credit card account) into the nonprofit's bank account at regular intervals. In most cases, there is an intermediary service called an automated clearinghouse.

The advantages of EFT are obvious: a predictable number of donor dollars ends up in the nonprofit's accounts on a regular basis and may be used immediately. In addition, EFT reduces solicitation and processing time, paperwork, postage costs, and many other administrative costs. One of the less obvious advantages of providing an EFT option for donors is that doing so may increase the dollar amounts of individual donations, as people are less likely to feel the impact of the moneys they are donating if they are not physically preparing a check and mailing it every month or quarter. This same logic may be applied to the duration for which individual donors support the organization. When people have to take action to *stop* their cash outlay (as opposed to being passive and allowing it to continue), they are less likely to discontinue it. Requesting regular increases of a few dollars at a time is also made easier and more palatable when money is already being forwarded without any action required by the donor. Finally, EFT via bank account or credit card can be administered over the Internet.

Organizations interested in starting an EFT program should contact their bank or credit card company directly to inquire about EFT services. Services are also available through third-party originators, which will administer the transactions for a small start-up fee and a percentage of the total transactions. However, it should be noted that many of these services require a minimum number or dollar amount of transactions.

Soliciting EFT donations will require a modified fundraising approach. Specifically, solicitations should inform potential donors about how this particular type of giving will help the organization achieve its objectives and how the EFT will work. They should also include suggested amounts or frequency of donations and enrollment information. Of course, contact information should be supplied in case donors have questions about the program.

2. The Internet

Organizations that depend on contributions for support should offer donors the convenience of making donations on-line. In fact, organizations that do not have a Web presence risk becoming invisible to a substantial number of donors. To put it briefly, there are many Internet users with a lot of money who are looking for good places to donate it on-line. Organizations that do not offer on-line donation as an option will be passed over by individuals who demand this convenience. Aside from the benefit of increased opportunities for fundraising, offering on-line contribution options will likely reduce fundraising expenses. On-line fundraising can result in heightened efficiency and will allow organizations to have a more favorable program-to-overall-expense ratio. Organizations that would like to add on-line contributions to their Web site (or that need to develop a Web site) should consult appropriate experts. E-commerce has many aspects to it and many options for services, so it is extremely important to get a knowledgeable and experienced consultant to ensure a successful entry into this forum.

Another way in which contributor-funded organizations may use the Internet to increase cash flow and reduce expenses is to conduct fundraising drives using e-mail for solicitations or to provide donors and potential donors with newsletters. This method of communication will save the organization expenses associated with postage, paper, printing, and so on.

E. Additional Considerations

One other possible consideration for nonprofits that receive a high volume of contributions by mail is obtaining lockbox services. Lockbox services, usually offered by banks, allow organizations to set up a P.O. box to which donors send their donations. The bank retrieves the mail from the P.O. box, opens the envelopes, makes copies of their contents, deposits the funds, and generates a report for the organization detailing all transactions. Other services, such as assisting organizations in acknowledging contributions, may also be combined with lockbox services. Lockbox services can eliminate a lot of the time and resources needed to process mailed-in funds.

The benefits of lockbox services are obvious: they are inexpensive, they provide an automatic layer of internal control, and organizations do not have to devote staff time to opening envelopes, depositing checks, and so on. The drawbacks are that there is a minimum volume to subscribe that may be too high for smaller organizations and that lockboxes may require a lot of planning to implement.

CHAPTER 14 Income from Grants

Successfully managing cash flow may be the most labor intensive for organizations that depend on grants for a substantial percentage of their funding. In addition to the cash flow management tasks that will be necessary for most nonprofits, grant-funded organizations must meet all of the procedural and other requirements of grantors. Organizations that depend on grants from more than one source (or multiple grants from the same source) must have systems in place to ensure that all of the requirements of each grant and funding source are met. Failure to comply with even one requirement might mean disallowance of funds or revocation of the grant, which could seriously affect an organization's cash flow.

Organizations that manage to follow all the rules and regulations related to their grants are rewarded by having one of the most stable of all income streams. Once a grant is won, the moneys are committed, and all requirements are met, organizations can rely on eventually receiving a cash inflow (with some exceptions, of course). Moreover, when organizations renew the majority of their grants yearly and have a history with their grantors, fairly accurate projections of the timing of funding can be made.

There are many types and subtypes of grants, each with unique funding characteristics and specific requirements. Entire volumes have been written on navigating each of the major types of grants, so, obviously, our coverage of this topic will be at the most basic level. Some of the major cash flow issues, obstacles, and strategies applicable to income from grants are summarized in Exhibits 14.1 and 14.2.

A. Private Sector Grants

Private sector grants can run the gamut in terms of restrictions on their use and other requirements. Without guidance or regulation, private grantors may require whatever they see fit of grant recipients before or after disbursing funds. Sometimes private sector grants may make absolutely no procedural demands of grant recipients. In the following subsections, we have divided private sector grants into three classes, based on the rigor of their requirements or restrictions. (Note that these categories are somewhat arbitrary in that there are many grants that overlap or fall between the levels of restriction described.)

EXHIBIT 14.1	Grants: Key Cash Flow Issues and Common Pitfalls

KEY ISSUES

• Educating all staff who will be responsible for administering grants about relevant grantor requirements.

• Establishing systems to ensure that all grant requirements are understood and fulfilled in a timely and appropriate manner.

• Maintaining ongoing communication with grantors so that your organization can develop accurate projections of when grants will fund and of any changes in grant status.

COMMON PITFALLS

• Failing to comply with grantor requirements, resulting in delays in grant funding or revocation of grants.

• Failing to obtain accurate information regarding the timing or amount of grants, resulting in failure to budget properly for grant funds.

• Failing to budget properly for grant funds, resulting in surpluses that may have to be returned to grantors.

• Failing to properly administer grants, resulting in adverse audit findings.

• Failing to properly plan for grant expirations by having alternative funding lined up.

• Failing to expend funds in accordance with budget guidelines, resulting in questioned or disallowed costs.

• Failing to adhere to cost principles required for government grants, resulting in disallowed costs.

1. Unrestricted Grants

Unrestricted grants are, in essence, no different from contributions. They may be used by the grantee to support overall operations. The grantor does not identify specific services that must be supported by the grant, nor are there significant reporting requirements. An example of this type of grant might be a corporation making a $5,000 grant to a local nonprofit to use in its operating budget without any specific performance requirements.

2. Targeted Grants

Targeted grants are given to the grantee with a designated purpose for their use (for example, to perform a service or to purchase a necessary type of supply or material). The organization may only use the grant moneys in the course of fulfilling the grant's stated purpose. Grantors of targeted grants do not usually specify the desired result of the service or purchase, except in general terms. Additionally, grantors often do not stipulate that the organization achieve a specific service- or purchase-related goal. Many of these grants do, however, require some sort of reporting or analysis of the use or outcomes

EXHIBIT 14.2   Grants: Cash Flow Problems and Solutions

PROBLEMS

1. Budgeting for a first grant and not being familiar with the grantor's requirements or compliance standards.

2. Grant funding is dependent on circumstances beyond your control.

3. Cash flow problems related to the administrative costs of complying with funding-source requirements.

4. Ineligibility to apply for or to receive certain types of grants because your organization does not offer the scope of services specified by the grantor.

SOLUTIONS

1. Budget conservatively. If possible, make sure grant moneys are not budgeted for essential services that will be compromised if the grant comes in late or fails to materialize. Make sure there are other sources of cash that might be used in such a situation. Also, it might pay to ask other organizations that have been recipients of a particular grant about how closely the grantor follows schedules and compliance standards.

2. Budget carefully. When grants are also dependent on other circumstances (such as the grantor itself receiving funding), organizations should be especially careful of how the grant moneys are budgeted. As in item 1, grant moneys should not be budgeted for essential expenses when receiving the grant is not guaranteed. Organizations that find themselves in this position must do all they can to make an accurate assessment of whether and when they will receive the grant so that they can budget accordingly.

3. Ask grantors for moneys for specific program administration purposes (such as recruitment of volunteers, purchasing computers, or training) or fundraising. (Government grants may not be used for fundraising expenses.)

4. Seek out joint ventures with other nonprofits for the purpose of applying for grants that specify a greater scope or number of services than either organization can fulfill by itself. For example, grants that specify the delivery of comprehensive teenage parenting services may be received by a consortium of organizations that can jointly provide prenatal care, counseling, and pediatric services.

of the grant. An example of this type of grant might be one that is given to a nonprofit after-school center by an arts foundation to benefit the nonprofit's summer theater program. The only requirements of this grant might be that the nonprofit must use the moneys to carry out the designated program, that the grantor must be told how the moneys are spent, and that the nonprofit must inform the grantor of the results.

3. Restricted Grants

Restricted grants are grants that stipulate the grant moneys must be used for a specific purpose, in a specific manner, and that impose specific reporting requirements.

Generally, grantors of these types of grants will identify the particular goals of the grant and the expected results, often in quantitative form. Restricted grants usually require organizations to keep track of grant-related expenditures with attention to detail and with adequate documentation. Also, specific types of reporting and analysis are required to sustain the grant. An example of this type of grant would be a foundation granting $100,000 to an organization that serves the homeless for its "meals on wheels" program, with the requirement that five hundred nutritionally balanced meals must be delivered monthly, that social service agency contacts must be provided, and that homeless people within a two-mile radius must be approached monthly to participate.

Note

It is important that relevant staff of all organizations receiving grants understand the special conditions, if any, that affect the management of grant funds and grant-related activities. For example, cost reimbursement grants, whether from private or government sources, only disburse funds to organizations when there are expenses related to the grant's purposes. Therefore cutting back on grant-related expenses will decrease both the amount of the grant and total cash inflow. Of course, we are not suggesting that organizations should budget more money than is necessary to fulfill the grant's objectives just to get reimbursed. We are suggesting that your organization should carefully monitor all grant income and related expenses to ensure that the organization is spending and accounting for funds appropriately.

B. Government Grants

Grants awarded by federal, state, and local government entities are usually very demanding in terms of their requirements and specifications for use, documentation, reporting, and so on. Along with their grants, these granting entities often provide "laundry lists" specifying every aspect of the grant's administration—from the specific types of people the grant must benefit, to the educational background required of those who run the grant-funded program, to the exact forms that must be completed to monitor the grant. Organizations that fail to comply with these requirements risk major delays in receipt of grant funds or revocation of the grant altogether.

C. Cash Flow Forecasting, Planning, and Grant Budgeting

As stated previously, cash flow projection, planning, and grant budgeting can be the most predictable and accurate for organizations that depend on grant income for support. However, this will only hold true when such organizations can consistently and properly fulfill all grantor requirements. In other words, organizations may spend time and resources developing great plans and budgets and then fail to receive the grant because of noncompliance with regulations. Grantees should maintain proper communications with the grantor during all phases of the grant cycle. Grantees that fail to communicate effectively will be unprepared for changes in requirements, in the amount of the grant, or in the timing of cash receipts. Of course, when this happens, even the best of cash flow forecasts, plans, and budgets become worthless. Thus the most important aspect of cash flow forecasting, planning, and budgeting for organizations that depend on grants for revenue is making sure that every one of the grantor's rules is understood, that the grantor's requirements are fulfilled by the specified time, and that close contact is maintained with the grantor to avoid any surprises regarding the disbursement of funds.

Another important aspect of cash flow budgeting in grant-funded organizations is that budgets must reflect all applicable grant restrictions. There are some grants offered by corporations that have no specific requirements. "Here's the money. You don't have to do anything special for it." However, grants often come with restrictions and requirements, as described in the previous sections. Complying with these restrictions and requirements often involves some extra effort in making sure it is shown that grant funds are being used for their intended purposes. Without such documentation of compliance with grantor requirements, grants may be canceled or delayed. One way of reducing the chances of exceeding the grant budget or violating a grant use restriction is to require approval on certain types or amounts of grant expenses. For example, requiring the controller of the organization (who should be familiar with the grantor restrictions) to give signatory approval for grant-related expenses over a certain dollar amount may prevent unintentional violations.

We recommend that both the organizationwide budget and cash flow forecasts exclude grant funds that have not been formally approved. Including a grant that ends up being delayed or revoked in the organizationwide budget can cause major cash flow problems.

When budgeting for organizations that are predominantly grant funded, it is important to make sure that appropriate moneys are allocated for the expenses necessary to obtain such funds. Researching grants, writing grant applications, monitoring the use of grants, reporting on grants to the grant sources, and other grant administration activities may require a considerable amount of staff time. Making sure that these expenses are planned and budgeted for is important in effectively managing cash flow.

Another consideration is the timing of receipt of funds. For example, some grantors will give a portion of the grant moneys up front but then require reports before they disburse the next installment. Some require reports before any moneys are disbursed. Others will disburse funds monthly for six months and then stop payments for the remainder of the year. Management of cash flow requires that these timing requirements be considered in cash flow projection. It is crucial for organizations that anticipate receiving "after-the-fact" funding to plan for this cash flow situation. Other cash flow strategies, such as obtaining a line of credit, will have to be researched and implemented. The costs associated with compensating for the delay in funding will have to be paid by the organization in most cases. For example, governmental grants usually will not pay interest costs.

As a final consideration in cash flow planning, organizations should be aware of any limitations on the duration of the receipt of particular grants. Some foundations make specific time or quantity limitations on the amount of money they will provide for each grantee. Grant expiration dates must be considered in all aspects of cash flow planning. We suggest organizations implement a "warning system" so there is plenty of advance notice of when a grant is due to expire. In this way, organizations may come up with alternative funding and avoid having to modify programs or suffer cash flow problems. Generally, organizations cannot afford to grow complacent and expect to be funded by the same source indefinitely.

D. Cash Flow Reporting, Monitoring, and Analysis

Cash flow reporting for grant income will require that organizations consider the same factors they must for grant income budgeting and planning. The most important of these factors will be full compliance with grantor requirements. It is extremely important for organizations that depend on grant revenue for support to review all accounting and reporting requirements so that these can be incorporated into cash flow management. We suggest a table or checklist be constructed for each grant, detailing all relevant information pertaining to the grant. The checklist should, at minimum, list and describe the actions and corresponding timetables for fulfilling all grant requirements. (See Resource B for a sample grant checklist.)

When organizations fail to comply fully with all grantor and other government audit requirements, there can be many dire consequences. Aside from cancellation of the grant, organizations can face penalties when they intentionally or unintentionally run afoul of laws and procedures related to the grant. Moreover, organizations that receive grants may be subject to complex audits from different sources. Audit findings that indicate noncompliance with grant regulations can end up costing organizations a lot of money to remedy. In addition, such audit findings or other serious compliance lapses can expose organizations to bad publicity.

When all rules are adhered to and proper cash flow planning and budgeting have taken place, there should be little variation in cash flow. However, this does not mean that organizations can be lax in their monitoring and analyses concerning grant cash flow. Many grantors, as part of their requirements, specify the types of monitoring recipients must perform and on which they must report. Organizations (and grantors) that want to ensure funds are being used in the best possible way must monitor and analyze how grant funds are being spent. One of the most useful analytic tools in financial management of grant funds is a budgeted-versus-actual analysis of expenses and income related to the grant.

Note

The Budget-Building Book for Nonprofits (by Murray Dropkin and Bill La Touche; Jossey-Bass, 1998) contains a number of different ideas and examples of budgeted-versus-actual reports. Budgeted-versus-actual analyses of expenses and income related to the grant should be performed on a monthly basis to allow for necessary and timely modifications to cash flow forecasts.

E. Cash Flow Technology Issues

The most important technology issues related to grant cash flow involve maintaining communication and managing data at the highest levels of efficiency. This will involve at least two technological areas:

1. *Information technology systems,* such as collection of grant income and expense information, entry of this information into computer systems, integration and analysis of the information, reporting of the information, and distribution of the information

2. *Communication systems,* such as systems to ensure ongoing updates of grant status and requirements and to allow for the rapid return of requested information, including e-mail, intranets, and Web site access

Ideally, organizations will have technological systems in place supporting other aspects of their operations that can serve many of the functions just described. Thus the challenge in managing grant cash flow will be in developing ways to use existing systems to meet informational and analytical needs. When current systems are insufficient for the purposes of managing grant cash flow, organizations will have to consider modifying them. Organizations must have technology in place to support all efforts to comply with grant requirements, such as budgeting, monitoring, reporting, and analyzing, and to maintain open communication with grantors.

Another consideration in cash flow technology related to grants, especially in organizations that receive federal funding, is having specific technology in place to address the special requirements of the federal government. For example, federal grants often come with reams of forms and attachments, and instructions for completing and returning them must be followed precisely. Having EFT capacity will be necessary for the administration of some types of grants.

F. Additional Considerations

An often overlooked issue pertaining to grants is how some organizations, in their efforts to remain compliant with their grantors, end up compromising their missions. This can happen when the grantee delays terminating an ineffective program or otherwise alters its operations for the sole purpose of staying in compliance with a grant. We have seen this happen in organizations that are primarily grant funded by long-standing, large grants. Unfortunately, the only way to avoid this problem in many cases is to consider alternative funding.

If there is one suggestion we can provide to improve cash management and the overall financial health of grant-funded organizations, it is to devote resources to strategic planning. Developing and periodically modifying five-year strategic plans—including anticipated changes in grant income and how these will be addressed—can go a long way toward keeping grant-funded organizations vibrant and ready for the future.

CHAPTER 15

Interest, Dividend, and Royalty Income

Interest, dividends, or royalties are rarely a primary source of income for the majority of nonprofits. However, income of this type can be a good supplementary source of cash because organizations do not have to perform services or generate major expenses to receive it. In the case of investments, the main challenges are raising the money to invest, investing for the greatest return, and making the best use of the investment income.

There are several different situations in which nonprofits may earn investment income. Some organizations receive contributions of stock from donors. In these cases, the organization's main task is deciding what to do with the stock (for example, to sell the stock and convert it to cash for reinvestment or use, or to keep it as an investment). Some organizations may develop policies requiring all donations of stock to be sold immediately, regardless of the relative value of the stock. In this way, organizations can avoid the time and expense of creating and managing a portfolio of investments. Of course, if the organization opts for this strategy, it could lose potential income when stocks it has sold go up in value. Obviously, the opposite could also happen: stocks donated to an organization can unexpectedly decline in value. Organizations that immediately convert stock to cash or more stable investments protect themselves from this outcome. Because of these risk factors, organizations should determine the amount of risk they can tolerate, the resources they can devote to portfolio management, and their short- and long-term cash needs before developing policies to handle donated stock.

Often organizations receive initial investment funds through contributions of cash. Capital and endowment campaigns are two examples of the ways in which organizations generate money for investment and future income. Sometimes funds may come with restrictions regarding the types of investments that may be bought with them and the ways the organization must use the income from the invested funds. Some of the major cash flow issues, obstacles, and strategies applicable to interest, dividend, and royalty income are summarized in Exhibits 15.1 and 15.2.

Each of the three types of income—interest, dividends, and royalties—has its own unique cash flow considerations, which will be addressed in this chapter. However, by far the most complicated aspect of planning and managing cash flow for this category of income is managing investments. Thus, although we will address considerations relevant to all three income streams, we will devote more attention to matters related

EXHIBIT 15.1	Interest, Dividends, and Royalties: Key Cash Flow Issues and Common Pitfalls

KEY ISSUES

- Reviewing your organization's financial status thoroughly to determine the best way to invest funds, given the organization's unique circumstances.

- Determining the amount of risk your organization can tolerate while still maintaining optimal cash flow and then investing (or not investing) according to this determination.

- Using investment or royalty income that has a high degree of certainty to budget for essential expenses.

- Monitoring the performance of all investments and modifying investment plans when investment performance becomes unsatisfactory.

- Reviewing the terms of royalty contracts carefully to make sure they are the most favorable possible.

- Comparison-shopping for the best interest rates on savings accounts, CDs, money market funds, and other interest-bearing instruments.

COMMON PITFALLS

- Choosing investments that are too risky and then being forced to dip into principal to pay expenses when the investments fail to produce the anticipated income.

- Failing to monitor both the financial status of your organization and the performance of investments so that the organization can make appropriate and timely modifications to optimize cash flow.

- Settling for less-than-ideal terms on savings accounts, interest-bearing investments, and royalty contracts.

- Failing to comply with any restrictions on the funds used for investing or on the income derived from investments.

to investment income. Following are descriptions and some basic information about the three income streams.

A. Interest

Organizations can earn interest income on several different types of investments. These include CDs, bonds, money market funds, savings accounts, and certain types of checking accounts. Even the smallest organizations will likely be receiving some amount of interest income. Interest income is most often earned at a fixed rate (with a few exceptions) and will be fairly easy to project for cash flow forecasts. Expenses associated with earning interest income include account maintenance fees for savings and checking accounts, transaction fees for buying CDs, bonds, and money market funds and, possibly, fees for outside financial consultation or portfolio management.

EXHIBIT 15.2	Interest, Dividends, and Royalties: Cash Flow Problems and Solutions

PROBLEM

1. Difficulty in determining what to do with a donation of securities.

SOLUTION

1. Assess the amount of risk your organization can tolerate. For some organizations, such as those with few assets or investments, selling the securities promptly is often the most prudent course. Generally speaking, nonprofits should be risk averse. The majority of non-profits will benefit from reinvesting funds from riskier donated instruments in lower-risk investments, such as treasury bills, CDs, certain types of bonds, and money market funds. For organizations that have enough invested to ensure a margin of safety, investing a small portion of funds in some higher-risk instruments might allow for increased returns. However, the majority of funds should always be in low- or no-risk instruments to protect the organization against any bad high-risk investments. (Note that state laws may govern the types of investments used for certain endowment funds.)

B. Dividends

Organizations can earn dividends when they have investments that include securities, such as stocks and mutual funds. This income stream is less predictable than interest income because dividends vary based on the economic performance of individual companies. The major expenses associated with dividend income involve transaction fees for purchasing the securities and fees associated with obtaining investment advice.

C. Royalties

Royalty income may be earned from the sales of publications and other types of media, including books, compact discs, audiotapes, and videotapes, when the organization was involved in the creation of the materials. Royalty income may also be earned from "affinity cards" (credit cards that carry the organization's name and pay a percentage of each purchase to the organization). Royalty income is performance based; therefore it is not always predictable. Income will correspond to the amount of items sold or the number of transactions made with an affinity card.

D. Cash Flow Forecasting and Planning

Cash flow forecasting and planning will vary considerably, depending on the percentage of its total income an organization receives from interest, dividends, and royalties. For organizations in which these income sources account for less than 5 percent of total income, we suggest that the moneys not be budgeted at all. Rather, they should be put in a reserve fund for emergencies or for planning or starting new programs. Of course, the money may also be used to bolster the organization's overall financial strength.

Organizations that earn a substantial amount of money from interest, dividends, or royalties will of course have to project and plan for the money as they would for any other income source. In terms of income projection, using historical data will be the most practical way of figuring future income. For example, organizations that have invested in mutual funds will have to look at the performance of the funds over the past five years to project income from that source. Industry averages and projections are also useful tools for arriving at a more accurate income projection. Obviously, when dealing with fixed-interest-rate income, creating cash forecasts is a straightforward task. Simply multiplying the principal by the interest rate indicates the amount of income you will receive. Determining when the income will be available or when it will be received is the only other information you will need in order to project cash flow for this income stream.

Projecting royalties can be a little trickier. Obviously, if the royalty situation is a new one, it will be difficult to predict income. Thus, anticipated income should be set aside as an emergency reserve. Conversely, if your organization has established a historical precedent for earning a certain amount of royalties, this should be used to project income. Certain industries, such as the publishing industry, pay royalties according to the terms of particular royalty contracts. Make sure your organization reviews all royalty contracts to determine the timing and frequency of royalty income.

Planning and forecasting cash flow for interest, dividend, and royalty income should be done very conservatively, unless the income is guaranteed, which will be true of instruments like savings accounts and CDs. Guaranteed income may be budgeted for essential expenses. However, all uncertain income should be budgeted for nonessential expenses. In addition, when budgeting income earned from an endowment, organizations must be very careful to comply with all restrictions, regulations, and reporting requirements.

E. Cash Flow Reporting, Monitoring, and Analysis

The most important aspect of cash flow reporting, monitoring, and analysis for the income streams discussed in this chapter is consistently receiving updated data on actual cash flow versus projected amounts. If you receive interest income from a savings account, for example, it means reviewing monthly bank statements to ensure that rates remain favorable. If your organization has invested in CDs and bonds, it means being prepared for when they mature by having a plan for the funds.

Analyses of interest-bearing investments will obviously include comparison against equally safe investments. When these comparisons reveal that your organization could be earning more interest if it moved its funds elsewhere, options should be studied and, if desirable, implemented. About once a month, the newspapers describe a case in which a church or other organization has been defrauded in an investment scam. If an investment seems too good to be true—for example, if you are told that the interest your organization will get is more than a quarter- to a half-point above the interest a reputable bank would pay—it virtually has to be a fraudulent scheme. Credit markets are linked and in constant adjustment. Watch out for that "friend" who has a "deal" for your organization.

For dividend-bearing investments, such as common stock, organizations should receive and review regular (at least monthly) updates on the status of the investments. Many brokerage firms offer phone and Internet account services so that organizations can monitor their investments more closely. Analyses of dividend-bearing instruments should include comparisons against other instruments with a similar degree of risk. Also, industry benchmarking statistics should be used to help organizations determine if their investments are performing well.

Of course, anytime an organization is involved in investing, it should make sure it is obtaining competent and experienced advice. Unless "dabbling in the market" is part of your mission, it is unlikely that any staff member will have the requisite knowledge and expertise to effectively manage investments, especially securities. Organizations must solicit the input of their board's investment committee whenever making investment decisions or seek the advice of an experienced investment adviser.

Note
State laws may govern the types of securities organizations may purchase with endowments and other permanently restricted net assets.

When receiving royalties, organizations should review royalty statements and take note of any changes in income, especially decreases. When royalty income appears to be moving downward, organizations may want to review promotional efforts for the products earning the royalties. Often a change in advertising strategy will be enough to increase income. Organizations may also want to periodically compare their royalty agreements against industry norms to ensure that they are maintaining the most favorable terms. When accounting for royalty income, organizations should review the latest IRS guidance on such income, especially concerning income earned through affinity credit cards.

F. Cash Flow Technology Issues

The technologies most helpful in managing this income stream are those that will facilitate communication with the banks and brokerage firms holding the organization's assets. For example, the Internet will allow access to the most current information on the organization's investments. Also, such technology will provide an efficient avenue for researching performance and identifying other options for investing.

The other type of technology that will be important in optimizing cash flow in this area is information management systems. Organizations that have a substantial portfolio of investments should consider investing in software to manage investments. Portfolio management software programs contain templates for manipulating data relevant to investment income and money management. Furthermore, the organization's spreadsheet or database software should also be used for keeping track of investment and royalty information and generating monthly status reports and analyses. For smaller organizations or those without substantial portfolios, there are several Web sites that offer services for tracking investments economically.

G. Additional Considerations

In the majority of nonprofits, staff and board members have little or no experience in investment strategy, especially of the type that would be most beneficial to the organization. Therefore this is an aspect of cash flow planning and management for which seeking professional advice is extremely important. Unfortunately, the best investment advisers give priority to working with investments of large sums that will generate large fees. Until recently, organizations without a multimillion-dollar portfolio had a great deal of difficulty finding competent managers for investments. However, some bank trust departments and other financial institutions will now accept portfolios as small as $250,000.

A second important factor in being successful in this area is recruiting at least a few board members who have solid experience in dealing with securities. An investment committee should be created, with written investment guidelines based on the size of the portfolio and the needs of the organization.

CHAPTER **16** Income from Membership Dues

P rofessional organizations, alumni organizations, arts organizations, sports clubs, and fraternal organizations are among the types of organizations that solicit dues from members as a source of income. The overwhelming majority of dues-collecting organizations also depend on other sources of cash inflow, as supporting an organization with membership dues alone is usually not possible. Of course, there are exceptions to this, such as large professional organizations with tens of thousands of members that are supported primarily by businesses, which usually pay a greater membership fee than individuals. A number of these organizations can operate with membership dues as their only major source of income. The majority of membership organizations, however, must have income streams besides dues, to support operations. Fortunately, members can be an excellent and reliable source of additional income. Some of the major cash flow issues, obstacles, and strategies applicable to income from membership dues are summarized in Exhibits 16.1 and 16.2.

A. Opportunities and Considerations

Once an organization has spent the time and resources to develop a loyal membership pool, the opportunities to use this pool to generate income are abundant. After all, the members have already expressed their interest in supporting the organization and presumably have conveyed their trust in the organization's use of funds from membership dues. Organizations may use this interest and trust to their advantage by marketing relevant products to their dues-paying members. Although it seems logical, many organizations fail to capitalize on this "natural resource" to the fullest extent possible. For example, organizations that only offer for purchase a newsletter and a coffee cup with an insignia or other memorabilia may be selling themselves short. Improving cash flow for these nonprofits might involve investigating options for making available to members a wider variety of products and services. Some associations offer members a number of specialized publications, professional development conferences and materials, insurance products, and other products and services that can supplement cash flow.

Aside from the issues already mentioned, organizations for which membership dues constitute a part or all of funding will have three major cash flow concerns related to their income from membership dues:

1. Maintaining a pool of dues-paying members

2. Keeping the costs of soliciting and retaining members as low as possible and collecting cash from members as quickly as possible

3. Making sure all IRS requirements concerning income from membership dues are considered

B. Cash Flow Forecasting and Planning

Cash flow forecasting and planning for income from membership dues will be fairly straightforward. The most important factors in this area of cash flow management will be (1) calculating accurate estimates of the amount and timing of dues income from members and (2) making sure that opportunities to increase income through sales of products are used. One obvious way of projecting monthly cash flow from membership dues would be to develop a spreadsheet detailing when annual memberships expire so that annual dues payments can be anticipated. There are also software products available that are designed especially to aid in the financial management of associations.

Asking members to pay their dues with credit cards is also helpful in increasing cash flow and in cash flow planning. People who must act to cancel a membership will

| EXHIBIT 16.1 | Membership Dues: Key Cash Flow Issues and Common Pitfalls |

KEY ISSUES

- Keeping solicitation and membership maintenance costs low, especially those related to direct-mail campaigns.

- Generating enough additional income to support your organization.

- Keeping membership terminations low and continually replenishing retirements or resignations with new members.

- Making sure compliance with all relevant tax and other laws is maintained.

- Knowing the characteristics of dues-paying members so that dues and other products can be priced and offered accordingly.

COMMON PITFALLS

- Failing to maintain your membership base or to increase membership.

- Setting dues too high or too low.

- Spending too much to solicit and retain members.

- Failing to develop long-range plans for maintaining the level of income necessary to sustain operations.

EXHIBIT 16.2   Membership Dues: Cash Flow Problems and Solutions

PROBLEMS

1. Low rate of membership renewal.

2. Inadequate income from dues to pay for soliciting or maintaining memberships.

3. Lack of market penetration in soliciting memberships.

SOLUTIONS

1. Make sure your organization is offering members something worthwhile for maintaining their memberships. One of the least expensive and most effective benefits you can provide is a well-produced and informative quarterly newsletter. The newsletter should contain updates on all of your organization's activities and accomplishments. Newsletters may also include articles that are useful or interesting to members. Offering an excellent newsletter will address the most important factor in maintaining membership continuation—staying visible to members.

2. Perform a cost analysis on your membership operations. Are your expenses for soliciting or maintaining memberships too high? Are there practical ways of reducing the costs? Are your dues set too low? Many organizations have a tiered membership structure in which basic individual memberships cost a modest fee, second-level memberships entitling members to greater benefits cost somewhat more, and corporate or institutional memberships cost several times the price of the basic membership. Another dues structure we have seen organizations use with success is offering a restricted membership to students and new members, who receive limited benefits, such as a newsletter. "Full members" and corporations pay substantially more but also receive greater benefits, such as educational opportunities (in the form of conferences, for example). In addition, some organizations increase dues income by offering members the opportunity to join specialized "divisions," for which supplemental dues are charged. Structuring membership dues in any of these ways allows organizations to earn enough money from dues to support membership operations (or even to create income) without overpricing the basic membership for those of modest means.

3. Make sure your organization is known by the majority of potential members. This is where some initial investment in research and marketing is valuable. Does your organization have an advertisement in any newsletters or magazines related to its function or desired target membership base? Does your organization regularly attend relevant conventions, symposia, and meetings? If so, is it visible to potential members, and are there opportunities during the conferences for members to find out more about the organization? Is your organization visible in schools with programs that might be relevant to your organization's mission? Recent graduates in related fields may be one of the best sources of new memberships. A second way of increasing market penetration is to rent mailing lists and engage in a direct-mail or telemarketing campaign. Organizations that opt to take this route must be careful to keep their solicitations focused. We strongly suggest hiring a consultant if your organization is new to these methods of soliciting members and you decide to use these methods.

be less likely to do so than people who must act to renew a membership. When dues are relatively high, spreading out the payments over the course of the year may increase memberships and collections because members may be more willing and able to make smaller payments. This being said, the timing of payments of membership dues must incorporate considerations beyond what is best for the member. For example, many organizations arrange membership operations so that all memberships expire at the same time. We recommend this strategy, when possible, as it allows the organization a designated period during which it can turn its focus to the issue of memberships. Obviously, different types of organizations will have different considerations when determining the structure of membership campaigns.

In forecasting cash flow for membership dues, the key considerations are making sure your dues cover money both for seeking new members and for maintaining old ones. Creating a detailed and effective operating budget is extremely important in managing income from membership dues. When cash flow forecasts for income from membership dues are based on a comprehensive operating budget, they will be an indispensable tool in promoting fiscal health. Without such budgets detailing income and expenses related to membership operations, organizations may lose sight of the total amount of money it is costing to solicit and retain members. It is quite possible for organizations to go overboard in their spending to recruit new members to the extent that the cash outlay per member exceeds the dues being received during the first year of membership. Forecasting cash flow for membership dues will allow organizations to perform more effective cash analyses of their membership-related operations.

C. Cash Flow Reporting, Monitoring, and Analysis

There are two major considerations membership organizations will have when designing and implementing systems for proper cash flow reporting, monitoring, and analysis. The first is having tools and skills in place to create extensive databases for the most effective management of information. These databases should include all member information, both demographic and membership related. (Issues pertaining to technology development for cash flow reporting, monitoring, and analysis will be covered later in this chapter.) The second major consideration in cash flow reporting, monitoring, and analysis in membership-driven organizations is complying with all regulatory and tax-related requirements.

For example, the IRS considers membership dues to be nontaxable related business income as long as the membership benefits offered to members further the organization's exempt purpose. However, if members receive direct or indirect personal benefits (that is, tangible goods or services) that do not further the exempt purpose of the nonprofit and that are of more than nominal value, then that portion of membership dues is considered UBI and is taxable, which affects cash flow. Obviously, organizations must review member benefits carefully to determine if and how much they will be taxed for income from membership dues and must include any taxes in cash flow forecasts.

Analyzing the costs of soliciting and retaining members is essential for ensuring that organizations structure their memberships for optimal benefit. To perform a cost analysis of membership dues, all membership-related expenses must be identified— direct costs as well as indirect costs. Once these have been identified, calculations must be made of the total cost of soliciting a member and the total cost of retaining the member. The next step in the cost analysis will be developing an estimate of the average duration of membership, expressed in years. Once this figure is calculated, organizations can determine the yearly costs of both soliciting and retaining each member. The final cost estimate should then be matched against the yearly dues charged to the member, to determine the cost effectiveness of membership income. Organizations that fail to perform cost analyses and to monitor the costs of acquiring new members may find that attempts to expand their membership base have a detrimental effect on cash flow. Exhibit 16.3 is an example of how a membership cost analysis might look for a small membership-driven organization.

EXHIBIT 16.3	Sample Cost Analysis of Membership Solicitation, Retention, and Maintenance

SOLICITATION COSTS PER MEMBER:[a]	
Researching Potential Members	$10.00
Direct Mail	17.50
Providing Initial Membership Materials	5.00
Processing Initial Membership Payment	5.00
Allocated Overhead	12.50
Total Solicitation Costs per Member	**$50.00**
Average Number of Years Membership Retained	**5**
New Member Solicitation Costs per Year ($50 / 5)	**$10.00**
YEARLY MEMBERSHIP MAINTENANCE COSTS PER MEMBER:	
Newsletter and Insert	$4.00
Postage	3.00
Processing Membership Dues	1.00
Allocated Overhead	5.00
Total Yearly Membership Maintenance Costs per Member	**$13.00**
TOTAL YEARLY COSTS PER MEMBER (ACCRUAL BASIS)	$23.00

[a]Overall cost of member solicitation divided by the number of members successfully recruited.

Note

In the scenario in Exhibit 16.3, the actual cash outlay would be $40 higher than the $23 figure cited. For accrual accounting purposes, we only included one-fifth of the total solicitation cost to arrive at the yearly cost. However, organizations must take into consideration the actual cash outlay involved in getting a new member (in this example, $50) when forecasting cash flow related to membership dues. Using the figures from Exhibit 16.3, for example, if dues collected are less than $63, the organization will actually have negative cash flow in the year a new membership is acquired. (Note that $63 is the cash outlay for a new member—$50 plus the $13 outflow for membership maintenance.) Unfortunately, there are organizations that fail to understand this equation, attempt to expand memberships, and run out of cash in doing so. Organizations must make sure they have a source of cash to finance membership campaigns that is independent of the expectation of dues payment.

D. Cash Flow Technology Issues

As mentioned in several of the previous sections of this chapter, organizations that want to improve cash flow management related to income from membership dues will need adequate information technology to properly report, analyze, and optimize income from members. Perhaps one of the most important components of this technology is a database application that will be capable of manipulating many different types of information in formats that are readily usable for analyses and reporting. For example, organizations that can easily access the duration of their members' memberships and their histories of purchasing products or services will be able to develop better projections of future income. In addition, being able to manipulate this information will allow organizations to create more effective strategies for increasing income from members. One way an organization can do this is by sending direct-mail product catalogue updates only to members who have made prior purchases, thus increasing the potential response rate and saving on direct-mail costs.

Another area of technology that membership organizations will find beneficial relates to the processing of the dues payments. EFT systems, in which dues are automatically transferred from a bank or credit card account into the organization's accounts, can increase both the efficiency and the rate of collection of membership dues. EFT is relatively easy to set up. Banks and a number of fulfillment houses offer this service.

Efficient and inexpensive communication with members can be vital in maintaining good cash flow in membership organizations. Having the technology in place to operate a Web page (especially one that allows for secure credit card transactions) and to perform bulk e-mailings of solicitations, newsletters, updates, and so on, can streamline membership dues operations immeasurably. Obtaining the necessary software and hardware to perform these functions is not difficult or expensive. Engaging the services of professional computer or Internet consultants is nonetheless always a good investment.

E. Additional Considerations

Several considerations relevant to improving or maintaining optimal cash flow that were not covered in the previous sections may apply to organizations that count membership dues or other member income as a primary source of support. The following subsections detail the most important of these.

1. Maintaining a Positive and Popular Public Image

Nonprofit organizations are often in a position where it is desirable, appropriate, or unavoidable to take a public stance on important issues. In fact, the missions of many nonprofits almost demand such action when the issues are relevant to the nonprofit's purpose. However, nonprofits that count on the financial support of their members must also be careful to maintain values similar to those of their members. At first glance, it seems that this would not be so much of a problem. One would assume that members of an organization support the organization's mission and that any action taken by the organization would be in agreement with its mission. However, it can become troublesome when there is a particularly heated public issue that crosses ideological lines. Membership organizations that take a public stance on such matters risk offending members—sometimes to the point of losing them. Organizations for which this might be a factor must proceed with due caution whenever making public statements or taking actions that could be construed as supporting a potentially controversial position. The main question such nonprofits should be asking themselves is whether it is more important to the fulfillment of their mission (which includes maintaining fiscal integrity) to take a public stance or to remain neutral in the interest of retaining their members?

2. Offering Something of Value to Members

Membership organizations may be able to solicit members, and even to retain them for a year or so, merely based on the benefit of the member's affiliation. However, to retain long-term members, organizations must be offering something of value to the members in exchange for their membership dues. This need not be something of greater than nominal monetary value (in fact, it should not be, if the dues revenue is to be regarded as such by the IRS). Benefits such as newsletters (if well produced and informative), discounts on organization-sponsored events, and the opportunity to purchase services (such as insurance and travel) at a group discount are all nice privileges nonprofits can offer their dues-paying members. Moreover, all of these items can be promoted in an ongoing manner, which will fulfill another important objective: keeping the organization on the minds of its members.

3. Participating in Joint Ventures

Another way membership organizations can improve their cash flow is to partner with other nonprofits or for-profits in offering goods or services to members. Ideally, the joint venture partners chosen by the organization will have a complementary mission or offer services or products relevant to the organization's area of operation. Participation in a joint venture may also provide an excellent opportunity for organizations to offer their members added benefits of membership. Examples of such arrangements might be:

- A membership-driven public radio station partnering with an arts institution to offer members discounted exhibition tickets

- A medical association partnering with an organization promoting awareness of a particular health problem to join forces in sponsoring a direct-mail membership drive

- A police benevolent association partnering with a local children's center to offer members discounted children's sports programs

4. Advertising

Organizations that have a vehicle through which to generate advertising revenue may increase cash flow substantially. Selling advertising can be very lucrative and may be one of the least labor-intensive ways of earning income. For example, organizations may publish a monthly magazine and sell advertising space in it to businesses trying to reach the types of people likely to be members. We have worked with organizations that have sold advertising to companies wishing to publicize scientific breakthroughs to the organizations' members. Some companies will pay large advertising fees to have access to an organization's members for employment recruitment purposes. In each of these cases, a membership organization was able to supplement income by hundreds of thousands of dollars. When organizations use this strategy of increasing cash flow, it is essential to consult with financial and tax advisers. Such income is usually subject to UBIT, which could affect cash flow.

Income from Special Events

Special events can help improve cash flow in organizations that use them properly. Well-organized and well-planned special events that complement the regular activities of a nonprofit can provide an excellent source of income. Some of the advantages of using special events to generate income include the following:

- Special-event income is most often unrestricted, which allows organizations to use it for any purpose. Of course, if the special event is for a specific charitable purpose, the organization should use the funds for the purpose identified. For example, a special event to help flood victims is very clear in its purpose.

- Special events can create a lot of positive publicity for an organization. Such attention can attract more donors, volunteers, board members, and potential employees.

- Special-event funds are often immediately available, unlike grant or membership income. Organizations may not have to wait to use the money generated at special events.

- Special events can provide opportunities to collaborate with other organizations, which can result in improved networking and communication, sharing of resources, and other types of joint efforts.

Special events can also serve as a gateway for generating other types of income. Holding a special event that also functions as a membership drive, a contribution drive, or a service or product expo will allow organizations to potentially derive "three types of income for the price of one":

1. Income from sponsors of the special event

2. Income from charging event participants for their participation

3. Income from contributions, memberships, or sales of products and services

Special events may also have higher associated risks and can be more labor intensive than many other ways of generating income. Some risks and disadvantages of holding special events include:

- Up-front costs that are often greater than those incurred in other fundraising efforts

- Considerable time and attention devoted to planning and coordination
- The need to function in ways and areas that are beyond the scope of the organization's experience, knowledge, and comfort
- Risks associated with the event that could involve damage or injury to the organization, participants, performers, staff, service providers, and so on

Some of the major cash flow issues, obstacles, and strategies applicable to income from special events are summarized in Exhibits 17.1 and 17.2.

A. The Role of Special Events in Cash Flow Management

Special events can vary in importance to the overall operations and cash flow of an organization, depending on how they are used. There are many organizations that hold one or two special events per year to supplement revenue. An example of this would be a publicly funded radio station that runs a charity softball game in the spring and a brunch reception in the fall to kick off membership seasons. For other types of organizations, the special events may actually be a primary income-generating activity. This is true for some foundations and charitable organizations. Organizations such as these may hold "galas" during which participants are charged a per-plate fee and then asked

EXHIBIT 17.1   Special Events: Key Cash Flow Issues and Common Pitfalls

KEY ISSUES

- Planning, planning, and more planning—most special events, regardless of the scale on which they are conducted, will enjoy success proportional to how well they are planned.
- Keeping costs related to events contained so that the cost-benefit ratio remains favorable.
- Developing contingency plans for funding in case events are not as successful as anticipated.
- Using skilled and experienced consultants, especially when planning a new special event or making major modifications to an existing one.

COMMON PITFALLS

- Failing to properly troubleshoot and take action to reduce risks accordingly.
- Failing to obtain proper insurance, permits, licenses, and so on.
- Failing to attract sufficient turnout.
- Budgeting projected special-event earnings before they are received, especially when there is little history associated with an event to aid in income projection.
- Trying to do "too much too soon"—carrying out a special event can be very complicated, so organizations should learn to undertake special events gradually, starting with smaller ones and eventually working up to larger ones.

EXHIBIT 17.2	Special Events: Cash Flow Problems and Solutions

PROBLEMS

1. Some major event-related expenses must be paid prior to receipt of the majority of income from the event.

2. Not enough information to project income and expenses for a first-time event.

3. An event ends up exceeding expense projections and is unsuccessful at generating income.

SOLUTIONS

1. Ideally, organizations will know in advance when this scenario is likely to occur and will plan accordingly. However, there are some steps your organization can take to alleviate or prevent financial strain:

   a. Negotiate with vendors for timed payment options.

   b. Secure a short-term loan or move funds out of liquid investment accounts.

   c. Ensure that the event will be successful enough to pay all related expenses if your organization borrows money or obtains credit from vendors. The best way to deal with this issue is to require participants in the special event to submit any fees or payments before the event takes place. This strategy will ensure that cash flow remains stable even if an unforeseen or uncontrollable situation (like the weather) adversely affects your event. (Insurance is available to protect your organization from some of these catastrophes. Check with your organization's insurance agent for products that might be relevant.)

2. Budget conservatively. Organizations budgeting first-time event expenses and income must be as conservative as possible. Many variables can affect both sides of the expense-income equation, making projections seriously unreliable. Doing as much research as possible before the event will aid in preventing wild miscalculations. As mentioned elsewhere in this chapter, income from special events should never be budgeted to pay for essential operating expenses unless the event has a proven track record of consistent income and predictable expenses.

3. This problem represents the greatest fear of fundraisers—the fear that a special event will flop. Obviously, once this occurs, it is impossible to completely reverse the damage. However, if all of our previous recommendations are followed, then, ideally, the damage will not be too great. In the aftermath of a failed special event, organizations must use the opportunity to learn from their mistakes so that the next event will be more successful. In doing so, the following steps are essential:

   a. Perform a thorough review of all aspects of the event to determine why it failed. When doing this, organizations should solicit the input of people who were involved in the event in different ways (such as staff, board members, participants, and volunteers). The information they provide can be invaluable in making the next special event more successful.

   b. Review your organization's planning processes and expense and income data related to the event with the goal of improving these aspects for the next event.

Note: Solutions 1a and 1b are likely to generate additional expenses that would have been unnecessary with better planning.

to make additional contributions. Obviously, organizations for which special events are one of many funding sources will have cash flow management considerations different from those of organizations that are predominantly special-event funded. However, there will also be some similarities in planning, accounting, budgeting, and other functions related to the special events themselves.

B. Special-Event Planning

Poorly planned events are very risky; they can cause an organization to lose substantial amounts of money and can damage its public image. In addition, poorly planned events are risky in the sense that they can allow something potentially dangerous to take place. The following are some suggestions for effective special-event planning:

- Organizations that are inexperienced in holding special events should start with a small event and make sure expectations are realistic in terms of fundraising. Events with fewer variables have fewer risks and fewer unexpected results. Also, holding a minor special event will serve as a valuable learning tool for planning larger future events.

- Solicit the support of the board and the community while planning the event. Their involvement in such tasks as generating publicity for the event and recruiting volunteers to staff the event can be invaluable.

- If possible, hire an event planner. The expense of contracting with a professional will almost always pay off. This is especially true when a large event is being planned and the organization does not have a track record in holding larger events.

- Create an event-planning calendar. Event-planning calendars are essential to making sure all aspects of preparation for the event are completed on time. The calendar should specify dates for event-planning meetings, identify the various aspects of the event that need to be taken care of (with a deadline for each), and identify exactly what has to be done to complete these tasks and by whom. The calendar should also identify anything that might have an effect on the timing of preparations. For example, the dates when funding proposals are due should be included. The more detailed the planning calendar is, the better the chances are that preparations for the event will go smoothly.

C. Cash Flow Forecasting and Planning

There are two very different phases to cash flow forecasting and planning for special events. The first phase occurs before the event takes place, when, in most cases, there will be more cash outflow than cash inflow related to the event. Many vendors, performers, and others who must be paid will require payment in advance or on the day of the special event. Thus pre-event cash flow forecasting and planning will be focused on meeting event-related expenses. The second part of the forecasting and planning process will be focused on meeting postevent expenses and managing the income received from the event.

1. Development of a Cash Forecast

When projecting cash flow for the period before the event, organizations should develop a *cash forecast*. This document should contain descriptions, names and contact numbers, amounts, and due dates for each expense. To avoid cash shortfalls, it is essential that your organization plan thoroughly how it will pay for pre-event expenses. For example, if in the month prior to the event, $45,000 will be due to vendors and only $5,000 has been received in connection with the event, your organization may find itself in a negative cash flow situation. If this potential cash flow problem has been projected, your organization may divert moneys from other budget categories or use its line of credit to cover the cash shortage.

2. Postevent Considerations

Cash flow projection and planning for the period after the event will be primarily focused on collecting the income from the event and paying off remaining expenses. As we have mentioned at other points in this book, when projecting income that is not definite, the funds should not be earmarked for essential cash outflows, such as payroll, office rent or mortgage, utilities, and so on. Often special-event income will not be assured or easy to project and will fall into the category of indefinite. The degree or proportion to which this is true will depend on the history of the event. If your organization has been running the same event for ten years and has been receiving approximately the same amount of income from the event every year, a substantial proportion of those funds may be included in the budget as definite and may be used for essential expenses. However, when your organization is holding an inaugural special event or one without much history, very little of the projected income should be included as definite in the budget. This formula should be followed no matter how well the event is planned.

3. Opportunity Budgeting

One ideal way to budget income received from special events, especially the portion that is categorized as indefinite, is to include it in an *opportunity budget*. In simple terms, opportunity budgeting is budgeting that incorporates the concept that organizations should have funds set aside to take advantage of unique opportunities that might arise. These opportunities might include a chance to expand a program or to make an unexpected but beneficial purchase with highly favorable terms. Using opportunity budgeting for uncertain income from a special event will prevent the cash flow problems that can sometimes arise when such funds are budgeted for essential expenses. (For more information on opportunity budgeting, see *The Budget-Building Book for Nonprofits* [by Murray Dropkin and Bill La Touche; Jossey-Bass, 1998].)

D. Cash Flow Reporting, Monitoring, and Analysis

Cash flow reporting, monitoring, and analysis can become quite complicated for special events, especially if several are held per year. This is due to all of the reasons previously listed, as well as some others. One complicated aspect of cash flow accounting related to special events concerns the different types of income that might be received in conjunction with the event. For example, special events may generate income from contributions, sales of inventory or services, membership dues, and payments for admission. This can be tricky because some of these types of income might carry restrictions and some might involve special accounting steps required by regulatory bodies, such as the IRS. We suggest that organizations develop accounting procedures that will address all of these special-event considerations, especially if events are held frequently or if they are large or complicated.

Note that income from "special" fundraising events usually qualifies for exclusion from unrelated business income (UBI) under the Internal Revenue Code. Certain types of fundraising events will fall into this category (see Exhibit 17.3).

Reporting, monitoring, and analysis of special-event cash flow should start with a spreadsheet identifying all event-related expenses and income, including overhead expenses allocable to the event. Each entry should include a description of the item; payment status (paid or owed and date paid or due); for income, any restrictions on the income; and any special reporting or accounting procedures that will be necessary for the item. With this type of information readily available, organizations will be able to effectively perform analyses of and report on event-related cash flow. This information will be useful both in modifying cash flow forecasts and operating budgets (if necessary) and in planning future events and budgets.

E. Cash Flow Technology Issues

Cash flow technology issues for special events will include those pertaining to managing event-related finances, plans, procedures, staffing, and participants. Most up-to-date spreadsheet and database software applications will be sufficient to manage small

EXHIBIT 17.3	Definition of Special-Event Income

"Special fundraising events" can include banquets, dances, auctions, and so on. Normally, they are not subject to UBIT if:

1. They are not regularly carried on.

2. Substantially all of the work involved is carried out by volunteers.

or medium-sized events. For more complex or regularly occurring special events, such as those associated with arts-related organizations, event-specific specialty software is available and would be a good investment. One of the most important aspects of special-event technology in terms of cash flow is good list management. Organizations must be able to effectively use lists of members, lists of prior participants, and other lists to ensure the best turnouts for their events. Many of the technology issues for special events will be similar to those for income from membership dues (see Chapter Sixteen).

F. Additional Considerations

Holding special events to generate income has many advantages over other types of fundraising. However, there are a few drawbacks as well. One such drawback that can seriously affect cash flow is the much higher element of risk associated with special events. The larger or more complicated the special event, the greater the chances are that something will go wrong. The risks that come with holding a special event are often greater and more far-reaching than most nonprofit managers realize. That is why it is important for every nonprofit organization that is planning a special event to perform a thorough risk assessment in the very early stages of planning. Special-event risk will fall into several categories:

- Risks related to economic loss, failure of the event, or inability to meet expectations for income

- Liability-type risks concerning participants in the event and those staffing the event, including risks of personal injury, property damage, and theft

- Risks regarding the organization's public image or reputation

One of the most important considerations in reducing special-event risk is choosing the location wisely. Keeping costs contained often means that your organization will not have access to the "ideal" facility for holding its special event. For example, a special event featuring live music would ideally be held in a concert hall with great acoustics, comfortable seating, close proximity to public transportation, and pleasant restrooms. Few organizations are in a position to secure such facilities (unless the space is donated). Thus organizations should have a list of priorities when searching for a venue, most of which should be related to reducing the types of risks listed previously. We believe the considerations shown in Exhibit 17.4 are among the most important.

The following are some other suggestions for reducing risks associated with holding special events:

- *Make sure proper controls related to cash collection and management are in place.* Unfortunately, one risk of holding a special event is failing to carry out cash collection control procedures to prevent theft or accidental mishandling. Cash boxes, ticket controls, and supervision of staff should all be a part of written control procedures that are distributed to all who are staffing the event. One of the best ways to control cash at special events is to limit cash

| EXHIBIT 17.4 | Suggestions for Reducing Special-Event Risks |

- The space should be large enough to hold the anticipated number of participants comfortably and all equipment, plus some additional room in case an error is made in estimating the amount of space needed. Obviously, if the event includes any activity requiring substantial space (such as dancing or sporting events), this must be considered. Overcrowding can substantially increase risks of injury and property damage. In addition, there should be an appropriate number of restrooms (including wheelchair-accessible ones) for the number of attendees expected. Proper heating or cooling capacity also should be verified.

- The venue should have enough well-situated and well-marked entrances and exits so that all participants will be able to leave quickly in case of an emergency. Also, organizations must consider the security of the attendees.

- The site should not contain any safety violations or hazards, such as slippery floors, unbarred windows (when children will attend), excessive debris, or insufficient lighting. The site should be equipped with standard safety equipment, such as smoke alarms, fire sprinklers, fire extinguishers, and a working telephone.

- Outdoor venues should include an area where people can go in case of excessive heat or cold.

handling to only a few people at the event. Using a voucher system in which participants purchase vouchers at a central location and then use them to obtain goods is one way of managing this strategy. In addition, a team of senior executives should double-check all cash receipts against control records.

- *Obtain all necessary permits well in advance of the event.* Such permits might include those for using a facility, space, or equipment or for performing an activity.

- *Make sure to obtain the proper insurance.* Often organizations will have to purchase additional insurance (beyond preexisting policies) to cover them for special-event risks. Different types of events will require different types and amounts of coverage. Organizations should consult with their insurance agent or administrator to ensure that proper coverage is in place prior to the event. In addition, organizations should require that all participating vendors show proof of proper insurance before signing a service contract.

- *Hire a professional event planner.* Event planners who are experienced in the type of event being held will be able to plan and execute the event with greater efficiency and effectiveness than staff members will. Competent and experienced event planners will also be a tremendous help in reducing risk. Furthermore, event planners may have access to reduced prices for event-related products and services.

CHAPTER 18 Real Estate and Rental Income

For the majority of nonprofits, rental income is not a significant source of cash inflow. However, for organizations that *are* significantly involved in real estate, effective cash flow planning and management of rental income is essential and can be very challenging. This should not prevent an organization from becoming involved with property management when it relates to the organization's mission. Nonprofits that operate housing facilities serve a vital function, often providing shelter to people who might not otherwise be able to afford this basic and perpetual need.

A. Challenges and Considerations

Real estate management requires a specific set of management skills beyond those required for general management of an organization. For nonprofits involved in low-income housing, the task is even more complex because of a greater number of regulations and restrictions concerning tenants, rent charges, and other aspects of operations. Moreover, tenants fitting the economic guidelines of buildings managed by nonprofits may present a number of additional unique management issues. Obviously, organizations that enjoy rental income from renting or leasing property they own to other organizations or businesses will have fewer and less complicated management responsibilities.

Cash flow planning and management will be very important to organizations that manage real estate. Some of the major cash flow issues, obstacles, and strategies applicable to real estate and rental income are summarized in Exhibits 18.1 and 18.2.

When real estate is involved, there is little room for error in cash flow planning and management. This is due to a number of factors that are either impossible to change or very unlikely to change. Primary among these factors concerns the fixed nature of many of the cash outflows associated with owning or managing rental property. For example, mortgages frequently involve an inflexible cash outflow that cannot be substantially reduced during the life of the project. Utility expenses are also a regularly occurring expense, as are security, maintenance, renovation, advertising, insurance, and real estate tax or payment in lieu of taxes (PILOTS). Also, the legal expenses that are often incurred in the course of managing property can be high. Evicting a tenant for not paying rent, for example, can involve large legal fees, in addition to lost rent that will never be recovered.

EXHIBIT 18.1   **Real Estate and Rentals: Key Cash Flow Issues and Common Pitfalls**

KEY ISSUES

- Containing costs so that they are as low as possible while still allowing for satisfactory upkeep (organizations must obtain the most favorable terms on insurance, building maintenance, supplies, security, and so on).

- Screening tenants as carefully as possible for their ability to pay rent in full and on time, for the likelihood that they will stay for the duration of the lease, and for the likelihood that they will take care of the property and not violate any terms of the lease.

- Complying with all applicable outside regulations, including those specifying tenant selection and screening processes, tenant rights and responsibilities, management rights and responsibilities, lease stipulations, rental amounts, record-keeping and documentation requirements, and requirements related to the physical property itself.

- Establishing effective administrative procedures to ensure prompt and correct third-party payment of rent, when applicable.

- Keeping occupancy as high as possible, which means that getting vacant apartments back in service must be a priority, both during initial leasing and upon apartment turnover.

COMMON PITFALLS

- Screening tenants poorly, leading to rent arrears, property damage, excessive turnover, and vacancies.

- Incurring high legal fees associated with eviction proceedings.

- Violating building codes, resulting in fines.

- Failing to collect third-party payments owing to poor administration.

The second major factor in managing real estate income is that the amount of rent an organization can collect from tenants is often strictly limited. When all units of a nonprofit's rental property are occupied, there may be no way of increasing rental income, aside from building more units. What this means is that organizations, as a primary concern, must make sure they are doing everything in their power to keep all available units occupied with rent-paying tenants.

B. Cash Flow Forecasting and Planning

Owing to the factors already described, cash flow forecasting and planning for organizations that rely on rental income will be quite straightforward. When the majority of expenses are fixed and when income may be variable but cannot be significantly increased, proper management and planning take on an especially important role in ensuring good cash flow. Organizations supported by rental income have little room for

EXHIBIT 18.2   **Real Estate and Rentals: Cash Flow Problems and Solutions**

PROBLEMS

1. Units staying unoccupied for too long.

2. High incidence of vandalism.

3. Rent roll insufficient to meet operating expenses.

SOLUTIONS

1. Make renting vacant apartments a high priority. Units that remain unoccupied are a huge cash flow problem: the income that might have been earned on the property will never be realized. To ensure that apartments are generating income again as soon as possible, your organization must perform, at minimum, the following tasks:

   a. Identify what must be done to the apartment to physically prepare it for renting, and determine how long the work will take to complete.

   b. Review any conditions on rental of the apartment imposed by outside agencies, government entities, or organizational policies.

   c. Notify the proper entities of the apartment's vacancy, and supply information concerning when it will be available.

   d. Submit any required documentation or paperwork as far in advance as possible (many regulatory agencies have administrative delays that can last several months).

   e. Advertise the property, or list it with real estate agents, when applicable.

   f. Perform the necessary renovations, maintenance, and refurbishing.

2. Make sure tenant screening procedures include obtaining references from prior landlords and verifying these references. To the extent legally possible, refuse rental to persons who are suspect or who have evidenced immaturity or irresponsibility. In addition, consider hiring security personnel, installing surveillance equipment, or forming a tenants' association to encourage self-policing.

3. Review real estate–related expenses to make sure your organization is getting the best terms and prices for services and materials. Expenses that should be included in the review are insurance, maintenance, security, supplies, appliances, service contracts, utilities, security services, waste removal, repair and renovation, and real estate advertising. Also, review all leases and regulations pertaining to maximum allowable rents that may be charged for units. Make sure your organization is receiving the maximum allowable rent for each unit.

making mistakes in cash flow forecasting and planning. When projecting income, organizations should develop a formula to use that specifically considers the effects of vacancies and uncollected rent. Also, income projection should always be on the conservative side. There is a great danger in optimistic projections and cash flow forecasts that reflect such optimism. When nonprofits that have overprojected income then fail to receive the rent, they may not be able to pay for essential expenses. Furthermore, once tenants fail to pay rent, it is difficult for organizations to recoup the money. For these reasons, we strongly suggest organizations that depend on rental income create substantial reserves during the planning of the project. In addition, reserves must be continually replenished so they can be used to pay expenses in times of higher-than-expected vacancy and to cover unexpected expenditures.

For organizations that depend on rental income, the most important strategy in projecting, planning, and forecasting cash flow is to fully understand all of the conditions that affect the apartments they are renting. For example, information on each apartment must be maintained and updated regularly. This should include such information as the minimum and maximum rents that may be charged, the expiration date of each lease, and the major maintenance work that is needed and when it will be performed. Organizations must also maintain thorough and current records regarding tenants, vacancies, and especially the status of any vacant apartments and when the organization expects the apartments to be occupied. This information will be essential in developing cash flow projections.

C. Cash Flow Reporting, Monitoring, and Analysis

A central concern in cash flow management for rental income will be proper designation and categorization of expenses and income, in terms of sources, amounts, and so on. This is especially important for organizations that must report this information to government agencies. Government agencies often require extensive documentation and reporting of expenses and other operational data. In terms of cash flow monitoring, analysis, and improvement, organizations should be producing monthly cash flow analyses. Such reports will allow organizations to assess whether or not cash flow is optimal and to take remedial action early when a problem is discovered.

One of the most important monitoring and reporting functions for organizations that depend on rental income is arrearage reporting. Organizations should be generating arrearage reports on a monthly basis and should then follow up promptly with all tenants who are in arrears. The sooner an organization acts on nonpayment of rent, the less money it will lose and the better chance it will have of recouping back rent.

D. Cash Flow Technology Issues

Management of cash flow for rental income can be improved immeasurably through the use of appropriate technology. Organizations that manage real estate must process large quantities of data. For example, an organization that runs a program for low-income housing might manage one hundred units designated for rental by working single mothers, twenty-five units for the mentally ill, and fifty single-room-occupancy units. The same organization might coadminister with another agency a senior citizens' building with fifty residents and might be developing another residential facility to house seventy-five disabled clients. In this case, the organization would need to manage data on three hundred units. Some of the information that would have to be on record for each rental unit includes demographic data on the occupants, who pays the rent and how, what other agencies are involved and in what manner, the terms of the lease, and records of rent payment, maintenance on the unit, appliances in the apartment, and vacancy status. Organizations also must manage data on insurance, taxes, utilities, building maintenance, and reporting requirements to other agencies. In order to manage such an extensive amount of specialized data, organizations will benefit from using record-keeping systems that are designed for property management.

Other technologies that will help rent-supported organizations improve cash flow are the same as they are for many types of income streams. Using bank lockbox services for collecting rent may be a good idea if a sizable number of apartments are being managed.

E. Additional Considerations

1. Effective Leases

Organizations that manage real estate or are in any way involved with property rental must pay due attention to the leases they require tenants to sign. Lease terms should be spelled out in clear and understandable language and in enough detail to provide a thorough understanding of both landlord and tenant rights and responsibilities. Your organization should have a representative go over leases with tenants before they are signed. In this way, any questions can be answered, and the concerns of both parties can be addressed. Particular attention should be devoted to explaining the terms for eviction and responsibilities regarding rent payment and upkeep of the apartment. One of the primary reasons for doing this is that if problems arise later, there will be clear expectations of the actions that will be taken by property managers.

2. Security Deposits

There are local laws in some municipalities concerning what must be done when a landlord receives a security deposit on an apartment. In some cases, laws require that the landlord deposit the funds in an interest-bearing account in the tenant's name until the apartment is vacated. Organizations must make sure they are complying with all regulations when handling security deposits. Some banks have special arrangements that allow landlords to deposit security deposits into the landlord's account but under the tenant's name. The tenant is then issued an IRS Form 1099-INT for the earned interest at the end of the year and receives accumulated interest less an account management fee when surrendering the apartment.

3. Competent Staff

One cash flow improvement suggestion that will always be effective is for your organization to hire the best on-site staff possible. A competent and professional superintendent will carefully watch the usage of supplies, will be alert to monitoring and preventing vandalism, and will help in getting vacant apartments rented quickly. Having a good on-site staff person is a front-line defense against cash flow problems.

4. Other Opportunities for Increasing Cash Flow

Another way organizations involved in rentals can increase cash flow, at least modestly, is providing washing machines, dryers, vending machines, and secure parking. These services will add to the appeal of the property and provide additional income.

A final cash flow improvement strategy for an organization involved in real estate is to research refinancing property at a lower interest rate if the organization is in a position to do so. Keep in mind that refinancing may only be an option for organizations that financed their real estate purchase through conventional borrowing from banks, as opposed to subsidized borrowing from government programs. Refinancing a mortgage at a lower interest rate will reduce monthly cash outflow.

Note

Refinancing transactions can be complicated. An organization seeking to improve cash flow through refinancing should consult its accountant, attorney, and bank so that alternatives can be analyzed properly.

5. Ideal Management Model

We have found that the management structure that works best for organizations managing real estate includes the following components:

- **Internal Administrative Office.** This central office handles the legal and administrative aspects of operations. Tenant inquiries, complaints, application processing, lease administration, and all other administrative functions are performed by the internal administrative staff.

- **External Building Operations Team.** Ideally, this team has responsibility for several different locations and for all operational aspects of building management, such as cleaning, repairs, and so on. It is responsible for inspecting apartments for damage and renovation needs when the apartments become vacant and ensuring they are put back in rental condition so that they can be rerented quickly. In addition, this team is responsible for supervision of building staff, such as superintendents and porters.

Income from Sales of Assets

Organizations will almost never count sales of assets as their sole financial support. Most often, organizations will derive income through selling non-inventory assets in the following situations:

- When they are given noncash contributions by donors or other organizations
- When they are selling their own property acquired in some other manner
- When they are selling securities

A. Sales of Various Types of Assets

Some of the major cash flow issues, obstacles, and strategies applicable to income from sales of assets are summarized in Exhibits 19.1 and 19.2. The remainder of this section discusses a number of important considerations regarding sales of different types of assets.

1. Selling Property Occupied by Your Organization

It has been our experience that sales of assets will most often be a cash flow concern for nonprofits when they engage in real estate transactions. Specifically, many organizations will eventually be in the position of selling a building they had acquired and currently occupy. This way of receiving income has become increasingly important in the nonprofit sector because of the recent growth in the real estate market in many areas of the country. Organizations that bought property twenty years ago are, in many cases, enjoying large gains in the value of their property. Also, many organizations are likely to have different needs for space or facilities than they had when they acquired property and will need to sell based on this fact. In addition, buildings that were bought years ago might have upgrading needs that organizations may not want to fulfill. Opportunities to sell property at a substantial profit and move to a more suitable space have motivated many organizations to reevaluate their real estate holdings. A recent human-interest story in the nonprofit sector featured a nonprofit that sold its head-quarters building for a huge profit. The organization was able to purchase a new building with the proceeds of the sale and then had enough money left over to create a large reserve fund for future programs.

EXHIBIT
19.1

Sales of Assets: Key Cash Flow Issues and Common Pitfalls

KEY ISSUES

- Determining whether or not selling an asset would be the most beneficial action for your organization in terms of cash flow.

- Projecting when income derived from the potential sale of an asset would be needed by your organization.

- Considering environmental conditions and variables (such as market fluctuations and future changes in value) to determine when and how to sell an asset.

- Researching alternatives for space if the asset is a building occupied by your organization.

- Researching investment options to get the best return for converted assets.

COMMON PITFALLS

- Failing to perform effective cash flow projections and, as a result, having too much invested in fixed assets to meet liquidity needs and to maintain adequate liquid reserves.

- Failing to observe forecasts for market conditions and thus allowing your investment to lose value.

- Underestimating the expenses of maintaining assets, causing cash flow problems.

EXHIBIT
19.2

Sales of Assets: Cash Flow Problems and Solutions

PROBLEM

1. Current cash flow situation makes selling assets unnecessary or not in your organization's best interest, even though market conditions are favorable.

SOLUTION

1. Do a five-year cash flow forecast to determine when the funds from sale of the assets will be most beneficial to cash flow. Then research market conditions to ascertain if a sale when the organization will need the funds will also yield an acceptable return. If indications reveal that market conditions will remain stable and favorable, your organization should sell the assets when it is most beneficial to cash flow. However, if the market is expected to become less favorable, your organization should consider selling the assets sooner for the best return and finding a low-risk, short-term place to invest the proceeds until they are needed.

2. Selling Investments in Real Estate and Securities

Somewhat less frequently organizations will be in a position to sell real estate contributed to them or in which they invested but do not occupy. In addition, organizations that hold investments in the form of securities will need to consider sales of assets in their cash flow planning and management. The most important aspect related to sales of assets, in terms of cash flow, is determining whether or not it is financially beneficial to sell an asset.

3. Determining Whether or Not to Sell a Building Occupied by Your Organization

Organizations that are trying to improve cash flow may find that selling a building they own will be an effective cash flow improvement strategy. To determine the cash flow effect of selling such an asset, the organization should complete a thorough analysis and projection of the changes in expenses and income that will occur as a result of the sale. The following is some of the information that might be included in a presales analysis for a building in which an organization maintains its offices:

- Yearly costs of maintaining ownership of the building:
    1. Mortgage (interest)
    2. Taxes or payment in lieu of taxes (pilot agreement)
    3. Maintenance
    4. Renovation

- Liquid assets potentially gained from sale of the building (minus expenses of selling)

- Potential for return on investment of liquid assets

- Yearly cost of renting space

- Associated expenses (such as locating space, upgrading, and so on)

Once you have performed this type of analysis, the data can be used to determine how selling the building will affect cash flow. Cash flow projections should be developed for both selling and keeping the property.

4. Determining Whether or Not to Sell Investment Assets

Organizations that must decide whether or not to sell investment assets, either donated or acquired by the organization, will have a less complicated task. Performing a return-on-investment analysis will yield the necessary information for organizations to make a sound decision. For example, if the organization owns a building worth $600,000 for which rental income is $100,000 annually and expenses are $25,000, the organization is earning $75,000 per year on its $600,000 of assets. This 12.5 percent return is probably higher than the organization could receive on any other type of low-risk investment. Thus the organization would probably be best served by maintaining its real estate holding. However, if the organization knew it had to invest an additional $300,000 in the building over the next two years to upgrade it enough to comply with building codes, its return on investment would fall considerably below 10 percent. In this case, selling and reinvesting the money in treasury bills, for example, might be a more prudent action.

In some situations, it may be possible to sell the property occupied by the organization and then become a tenant in the building, thereby maintaining occupancy. If the space is still suitable to your organization, this option may be one worth considering.

B. Cash Flow Forecasting and Planning

The most important aspect of cash flow forecasting and planning related to sales of assets is performing accurate cash flow projections to determine if and when liquid assets from the potential sale of fixed assets would be needed. The information obtained from such projections will be essential in guiding the organization in determining when assets should be sold and what should be done with the proceeds. In most cases, we recommend that organizations do a five-year cash flow projection. The long lead time is often necessary in planning the management of fixed assets for two major reasons: (1) an organization must ensure there is enough time to research and attain the most favorable selling position when value fluctuates with market conditions and (2) it is necessary to make sure funds are available when the organization needs them.

When an organization has decided to sell a fixed asset, it is important for the organization to perform proper cash flow planning, projection, and budgeting related to the proceeds from the sale. Your organization must decide whether the income will be used to increase reserve funding, to fund a new program, to invest in a different investment instrument, or for some other purpose. We strongly recommend that organizations in this situation consult an experienced financial adviser before reinvesting funds from fixed assets. Often there will be many considerations that are not immediately obvious to those without experience in this type of investing but that will nonetheless have a substantial impact on future cash flow.

Cash flow forecasting related to sales of assets should incorporate these three major considerations:

1. Cash flow projections for either maintaining the assets or selling the assets (as applicable) in both cash flow and operating budgets

2. The amount of proceeds from the sale of assets and how they will be used

3. Up-front costs of selling the assets or reinvesting the proceeds

The five-year cash flow projections generated to determine whether or not assets should be sold or maintained will be useful in cash flow forecasting. Obviously, the projections the organization will use depend on what it decides to do with the assets (either selling or holding them). When an organization has decided to sell assets, cash flow forecasting must be performed with great attention to detail in terms of what expenses will be incurred as a result of the sale. In the case of selling investment assets, expenses will usually be limited to the research, consultation, and transfer or broker fees associated with the transaction. However, when the sale is of a building the organization occupies, accurate projections take on greater significance because of the greater number of potential expenses. For example, cash flow forecasts will have to incorporate any fees associated with both selling the property and finding a new space to house the organization, which may include the following and more:

- Real estate agent's fees for selling property
- Transfer fees
- Attorney's fees
- Engineer's or inspector's fees
- Assessment fees
- Expenses for necessary renovations
- Fees associated with paying off an existing mortgage or applying for a new mortgage
- Title and lien search fees
- Filing fees
- Security deposits
- Moving costs

C. Cash Flow Reporting, Monitoring, and Analysis

Income derived from sales of assets will require a relatively straightforward treatment in terms of cash flow reporting, monitoring, and analysis. Organizations that sell assets will need to develop spreadsheets to track all of the associated expenses and income listed in previous sections.

The monitoring and analysis of income related to sales of assets will focus on maintaining a more favorable cash flow situation with the proceeds from the sold assets (in terms of return, safety, or liquidity). Such monitoring and analysis will involve comparison with other investment instruments and options, as well as determinations regarding optimal use of the funds.

D. Cash Flow Technology Issues

The technology necessary to properly plan and manage cash flow related to sales of assets includes technology supporting effective communication, funds management, and information management. The Internet can be used to research and track investments and to keep abreast of relevant news in the real estate market. Organizations can also advertise property they have for sale and look for new property to rent or buy at a wide variety of Web sites serving the real estate market.

The majority of organizations will not need to acquire additional hardware or software to manage information related to cash flow from sales of assets. Virtually any versatile spreadsheet program will be adequate for analyzing data and preparing reports related to sales of assets. Common commercially available financial management software should also be quite effective for performing analyses and handling other financial data management functions.

E. Additional Considerations

Organizations that are in a position to sell assets must maintain vigilance in monitoring the relevant markets for news, trends, and other factors that are likely to affect the value of the assets. Doing so will prepare organizations to sell assets at the time when the assets will command the highest price and offer the greatest return.

PART FOUR

Putting It All Together

PART FOUR PRESENTS the culmination of all the chapters of *The Cash Flow Management Book for Nonprofits*—a practical guide to and example of the implementation of a cash flow management plan. In addition, we offer our concluding thoughts on cash flow management in Chapter Twenty One.

CHAPTER 20 · Your Cash Flow Management Plan in Action

By the time you have arrived at this point in our book, you will have read about the many different aspects of and approaches to effective cash flow planning and management. We hope you will have achieved an understanding of the role of this essential element in the financial health of your organization. We also hope you will feel confident in immediately applying some of the suggestions we have provided to address actual cash flow problems in your nonprofit. Perhaps our greatest hope is that we have conveyed the importance of an integrated and collaborative approach to effectively plan and manage cash flow in the real world.

Creating a comprehensive cash flow management plan is what *The Cash Flow Management Book for Nonprofits* is all about. To illustrate how the concepts we have addressed might look in their practical application, we have provided the cash flow management plan developed for Universal Nonprofit, the medium-sized multiservice agency we have used as an example throughout the book. We hope this tool helps in conveying how our cash flow management theories, information, and approaches can improve cash flow operations in your organization.

A. Sample Cash Flow Improvement Plan: Overview

The spreadsheet we have developed as an example of an overall cash flow improvement plan (shown in Exhibit 20.1) is intended as a summary of cash flow improvement steps and data, using Universal Nonprofit's cash flow circumstances. Obviously, organizations developing cash flow improvement plans will need to include a much greater degree of detail for each aspect of the plan, which would probably be done at the next level of development. In addition, organizations should use the plan we have outlined to develop detailed work plans for each department or staffing area in the organization. The work plans should describe the specific cash flow improvement responsibilities of the individual department or unit and should identify the actions it will be expected to take in fulfilling the overall improvement plan. The sample spreadsheet includes (in column 10) the chapters in *The Cash Flow Management Book for Nonprofits* that provide the information most relevant to the corresponding activities and tasks.

EXHIBIT 20.1 Sample Cash Flow Improvement Plan for Universal Nonprofit

Goal: Monthly cash flow improvement of $150,000; annual improvement of $1.8 million

1 Task No.	2 Objective	3 Activity	4 Responsible Person(s)	5 Target Completion Date	6 Actual Completion Date	7 Annual Estimated Cash Flow Improvement	8 Estimated Profit and Loss Impact	9 Actual Cash Flow Impact	10 Helpful Chapters in This Book
1	Improve cash flow reporting.	a. Develop policies and procedures for weekly, monthly, and quarterly cash flow reporting and analysis.	a. Finance, CFO.	7/31/01		—	—		4, 6, 7, 8
		b. Implement ongoing preparation of cash flow forecasts.	b. Finance, CFO, administration, program staff.						
		c. Implement periodic review and analyses of reported cash flow data.	c. Finance, CFO.						
2	Improve inventory control.	a. Increase inventory monitoring to once monthly.	a. Purchasing.	3/31/01		$100,000	$100,000		12
		b. Compare records of inventory use or sales to stock amount.	b. Purchasing, administration.						
		c. Analyze necessary levels of supplies.	c. Purchasing, program staff.						
		d. Seek economies of scale in purchasing.	d. Purchasing, finance, administration.						
3	Improve collections of accounts receivable by reducing time for collections to sixty days (currently ninety days).	a. Implement electronic third-party collection.	a. Finance, administration.	4/30/01		$200,000			11
		b. Review methodologies used for collection.	b. Finance, CFO.						
		c. Identify benchmarks to reduce accounts receivable.	c. Finance, CFO.						
		d. Prepare a plan to achieve goals.	d. Finance, CFO.						
4	Collect past-due accounts receivable.	a. Engage the services of a collection agency.	a. Finance, CFO, CEO.	2/28/01		$75,000			11
5	Sell assets where appropriate to improve working capital.	a. Evaluate fixed assets to determine which can be sold.	a. Finance, consultant, CFO, CEO, board.	6/30/01		$800,000	$600,000		19
		b. Develop projections for cash flow impact of sales of fixed assets.	b. Finance, consultant, CFO.						
		c. Develop a plan to sell assets.	c. Finance, CFO, consultant.						

EXHIBIT 20.1

Sample Cash Flow Improvement Plan for Universal Nonprofit *(continued)*

Goal: Monthly cash flow improvement of $150,000; annual improvement of $1.8 million

1	2	3	4	5	6	7	8	9	10
TASK NO.	OBJECTIVE	ACTIVITY	RESPONSIBLE PERSON(S)	TARGET COMPLETION DATE	ACTUAL COMPLETION DATE	ANNUAL ESTIMATED CASH FLOW IMPROVEMENT	ESTIMATED PROFIT AND LOSS IMPACT	ACTUAL CASH FLOW IMPACT	HELPFUL CHAPTERS IN THIS BOOK
6	Improve grant and contract compliance, and improve grant cash flow.	a. Review all grant requirements. b. Develop a list of reasons for failure to collect cash. c. Develop a corrective action plan. d. Review grant and contract payment schedules versus actual for each project, and identify liability.	a. CEO, managers. b. Program staff and managers, CEO. c. CEO, managers, administration. d. Program managers, finance, administration.	8/31/01		$200,000	—		8, 14
7	Increase contributions from individual donors.	a. Develop a monthly newsletter. b. Recruit a board member with fundraising experience. c. Hire a fundraising consultant to develop a major gifts campaign. d. Implement the major gifts campaign. e. Increase direct mail to a quarterly appeal. f. Develop Web site capability for on-line donations.	a. CEO, development and fund-raising staff, board. b. CEO, development and fund-raising staff, board. c. CEO, board. d. CEO, development and fund-raising staff. e. CEO, fundraising staff, consultant. f. CFO, administration, consultant.	9/30/01		$400,000	$300,000		13
8	Reduce employee costs.	a. Have managers or staff submit job descriptions for every employee. b. Have top managers review job descriptions for redundancies. c. Make staffing modifications to reduce full-time personnel.	a. Program staff, managers, human resources. b. Managers, human resources. c. CEO, managers, human resources.	9/30/01		$100,000	$100,000		5, 8

EXHIBIT 20.1 Sample Cash Flow Improvement Plan for Universal Nonprofit *(continued)*

Goal: Monthly cash flow improvement of $150,000; annual improvement of $1.8 million

1	2	3	4	5	6	7	8	9	10
TASK NO.	OBJECTIVE	ACTIVITY	RESPONSIBLE PERSON(S)	TARGET COMPLETION DATE	ACTUAL COMPLETION DATE	ANNUAL ESTIMATED CASH FLOW IMPROVEMENT	ESTIMATED PROFIT AND LOSS IMPACT	ACTUAL CASH FLOW IMPACT	HELPFUL CHAPTERS IN THIS BOOK
		d. Analyze operations that can be outsourced, and determine if outsourcing some staff functions would benefit cash flow.	d. CEO, CFO, finance, human resources.						
		e. Implement outsourcing, and make necessary staffing changes, if appropriate.	e. CEO, CFO, human resources.						
		f. Review employee benefits, and research whether more cost-effective alternatives exist for supplying similar benefits.	f. CFO, finance, human resources.						
		g. Change providers of insurance, survivor benefits, and retirement benefits if appropriate.	g. CFO, finance, human resources.						
9	Improve use of banking services.	a. Institute on-line banking, including on-line payment of bills, account maintenance, and investment and brokerage services.	a. CFO, finance, administration.	6/30/01		$10,000	$10,000		8
		b. Consolidate bank accounts to reduce service fees and administrative costs.	b. CFO, finance, administration.						
10	Improve investment return.	a. Perform an analysis on long- and short-term investments to determine if the risk-return profile is optimal.	a. CFO, finance, consultant.	6/30/01		$10,000	$10,000		15
		b. Develop a plan for reinvesting current liquid or soon-to-be-liquid assets and for investing new funds.	b. CFO, finance, consultant.						
		c. Implement "current" parts of the investment plan as appropriate.	c. CFO, finance.						
	Total					$1,895,000	$1,120,000		

Note: Selling an asset will generate cash if the sales proceeds exceed any debt on the property, but if the property is sold for less than its book value, an accounting loss will be created, according to generally accepted accounting principles.

B. Sample Cash Flow Improvement Plan: Step-by-Step Guide

This section details how to develop and implement a cash flow improvement plan that corresponds to the spreadsheet in Exhibit 20.1.

- **Step One.** Have the CEO, CFO, and program and department heads (the "cash flow improvement team") meet to discuss development of a cash flow improvement plan. They should do the following:
  1. Decide on the dollar amount by which cash flow is expected to be improved and the date by which this is expected to be achieved, breaking this down into monthly cash flow improvement goals.
  2. Develop a cash flow improvement plan calendar, including, for example, the dates of future meetings of the cash flow improvement team and the expected date of finalization and implementation of the cash flow improvement plan.
  3. Develop major objectives for the cash flow improvement plan and enter them in column 2.

- **Step Two.** Have department heads meet with relevant staff to discuss the cash flow improvement plan and brainstorm activities and tasks that will help the organization meet major cash flow objectives, obtaining staff input on realistic time frames for completing activities and tasks. Then proceed as follows:
  1. Have the cash flow improvement team meet again to discuss and decide on which of the cash flow improvement activities generated by each program and department will be used.
  2. Enter those activities in column 3, corresponding to the major cash flow improvement objective each is intended to achieve.
  3. Enter the individuals and departments responsible for performing the activities and tasks in column 4.
  4. Enter the target completion date in column 5.

- **Step Three.** Have the CFO and finance staff analyze data and develop estimates of the expected cash flow improvement and profit and loss impact associated with each major objective. Then proceed as follows:
  1. Enter these estimates in columns 7 and 8.
  2. Have the cash flow improvement team meet to complete a final draft of the cash flow improvement plan.
  3. Submit the final draft to the board for review and approval.

- **Step Four.** Once the board has approved the cash flow improvement plan, do the following:
  1. Incorporate into the cash flow improvement plan any modifications suggested by the board and finalize the plan.
  2. Have department heads develop detailed cash flow improvement goals and activities for their individual departments, based on the overall goals and activities.

3. Have department heads meet with all relevant staff to discuss cash flow improvement activities for which they are responsible and to answer any questions.

- **Step Five.** Have the cash flow improvement team meet regularly to analyze data, check the progress of the improvement plan, and modify the plan as needed. As activities and tasks are completed, enter the actual completion dates in column 6.

- **Step Six.** Perform an annual review of the cash flow improvement plan, evaluating the success of activities and tasks in achieving cash flow objectives. Enter the actual cash flow impact of each major objective in column 9.

Note

The projected effect each cash flow improvement objective will have on the organization's cash flow, entered in column 7, should be developed conservatively and with consideration of the costs of implementing the overall cash flow improvement plan. The estimated cash flow impacts of all objectives should total the cash flow improvement monetary goal developed in Step One. Some organizations may want to include additional columns for identifying the variance between projected and actual cash flow impact and explaining any discrepancies.

Conclusion

Nonprofit organizations serve a vital function in our society. They represent a major economic force, employing millions of people and controlling substantial assets. The employees, board members, and volunteers associated with nonprofit organizations make an everlasting contribution to the well-being of our society.

Financial challenges can highlight the resilience and ingenuity of nonprofit organizations. Such challenges can also serve as a wake-up call, providing the motivation to retool management assumptions and practices. Organizations must focus on earning income to become financially strong and to continue fulfilling their missions. There is no way of avoiding this basic truth. Maintaining good cash flow and solvency is more than just a sound management theory. The most eloquent management theories ever developed will mean nothing to an organization that is on the verge of bankruptcy and cannot pay its bills. As we have said often in these pages, without cash your organization will eventually fail.

The cash flow forecasting, planning, and management processes we have discussed in this book are a key part of effective financial management. Many of the principles, theories, and concepts we have described also apply in a much broader context to managing your organization more effectively. Organizations that have in place the operational systems, leadership, culture, support, skill, and information to carry out effective cash flow forecasting and management will also have laid the foundation for effective overall management. In our opinion, both effective overall management and effective cash flow management are predicated on the following four aspects of sound management practice:

1. Collaboration

2. Flexibility

3. Information and knowledge

4. Forethought, planning, and an orientation toward the future

A. Collaboration

We have emphasized the importance of collaboration in effective cash flow planning and management often throughout this book. However, collaboration is such an integral aspect of both cash flow and overall management that we must make the point once again: the earlier and more intensively you involve all relevant parties in your cash flow and general management processes, the more effective the result will be. Many organizations take for granted the wealth of information and richness of different perspectives that exist "in their own backyards." By this we mean in staff members, in volunteers, in managers, in the board, in clients, in consultants, and in the community. Seeking the input of these collaborators can be invaluable in helping organizations to achieve their goals.

B. Flexibility

Flexibility can mean a lot of things in business and management—so many things, in fact, that it has become more of a buzzword than an important concept. We have a very specific idea about how flexibility, one of our underlying management tenets, fits into an overall picture of effective cash flow management. In this context flexibility means both the ability and the built-in mechanisms to react to environmental changes and a more general receptivity to alternatives and innovation. Opportunity budgeting, first described by Peter F. Drucker in *Managing in Turbulent Times* (HarperCollins, 1980) and discussed in *The Cash Flow Management Book for Nonprofits,* illustrates both of these ideas perfectly. Briefly, opportunity budgeting is the process by which organizations build into their budgets the financial flexibility to take advantage of opportunities when the opportunities present themselves. Thus opportunity budgeting provides the structure and the ability to be innovative and to react to changes in the environment.

Zero-based budgeting (ZBB), a concept also developed by Peter F. Drucker (*Managing for Results,* HarperCollins, 1964), is another good illustration of how flexibility can help organizations function more effectively. ZBB, detailed in Chapter Five, requires organizations to be flexible in reexamining all of their assumptions about existing operations. In doing so, organizations are forced to look at alternatives they may not have considered. This process by its very nature requires an openness to new ideas, to change, and to risk.

C. Information and Knowledge

Dynamic environments and increased competition for resources make it essential for organizations to stay informed. Nonprofit leaders must manage their organizations very skillfully. Organizations need to have the systems and structures in place for training staff on an ongoing basis. Organizations that can use the Internet effectively will find that they have a limitless and efficient source of information. Using the Internet effectively means that organizations will, on a regular basis, seek input from a variety of sources to increase their understanding of what is occurring in their environments. Taking full advantage of the Internet will also allow nonprofits to access important tools for increasing operational effectiveness. Even though Internet-based companies have declined greatly in their stock value, the Internet remains a great tool for non-profits to utilize.

Providing ongoing training to staff serves two main purposes: (1) it creates an environment in which learning and increasing effectiveness are valued, and (2) it provides staff with skills and information for improving operations. Both of these benefits are integral to a successful organization.

Finally, we want to acknowledge the importance of seeking outside consultation whenever feasible. Operating environments have grown more and more specialized, and engaging the assistance of people with specialized knowledge and experience is becoming more of a necessity than a luxury. This is especially true in the areas of accounting, taxation, financial planning, legal issues, technology, and fundraising. Regardless of how well informed and skilled your organization's staff and board are, it is essential for you to recognize when expert consultation is necessary. Organizations that have spent the time and resources to gather a team of competent, experienced, and appropriate consultants will remain one step ahead of the game.

D. Forethought, Planning, and an Orientation Toward the Future

The conditions under which many organizations operate often make it difficult to step back and look at the "big picture." Organizations must monitor their operations relative to what the community needs. Planning should be based on community and client needs, not just on what your organization can get funding to do. Both of these actions are essential to strategic planning, to cash flow planning, and to maintaining long-term success. Ideally, your organization will take the time and spend the money necessary to (1) perform research so that you have a thorough understanding of the environments in which your organization will have to operate, both at present and in the future, and (2) develop a five-year strategic plan that addresses long-range budgeting and cash flow planning and management considerations.

Organizations must integrate these four basic elements into day-to-day operations to achieve optimal cash flow. Collaboration, flexibility, information and knowledge, and an orientation toward the future must become part of your organization's overall culture and philosophy in order for it to fulfill its greatest potential. It is our sincere hope that your organization will do just that.

Good luck!

PART FIVE

Practical Cash Flow Management Resources

P ART FIVE INCLUDES checklists, sample forms, worksheets, and other tools to get your organization started in developing a cash flow management plan based on the strategies contained in *The Cash Flow Management Book for Nonprofits.*

RESOURCE A
Sample Cash Flow Reports and Forms

Contents

EXHIBIT A.1 **Sample Cash Flow Detail Report**

Universal Nonprofit
Cash Flow Detail Report
July 2000

DATE	DESCRIPTION	CASH INFLOW	CASH OUTFLOW	CASH BALANCE
04/12/2000	Opening Balance	$—	$—	$665,069
04/14/2000	Bills Paid		48,745	616,324
04/14/2000	Payroll		290,000	326,324
04/15/2000	Revenue	30,000		356,324
04/26/2000	Revenue	622,000		978,324
04/28/2000	Payroll		290,000	688,324
04/28/2000	Revenue	80,000		768,324
04/28/2000	Revenue	140,000		908,324
04/28/2000	Bills Paid		210,000	698,324
05/01/2000	Bills Paid		139,500	558,824
05/12/2000	Payroll		290,000	268,824
05/12/2000	Revenue	30,000		298,824
05/15/2000	Bills Paid		105,000	193,824
05/26/2000	Revenue	622,000		815,824
05/26/2000	Payroll		290,000	525,824
05/28/2000	Revenue	80,000		605,824
05/31/2000	Revenue	140,000		745,824
05/31/2000	Bills Paid		106,000	639,824
06/01/2000	Bills Paid		139,500	500,324
06/09/2000	Payroll		290,000	210,324
06/15/2000	Revenue	30,000		240,324
06/15/2000	Bills Paid		105,000	135,324
06/22/2000	Payroll		290,000	(154,676)
06/28/2000	Revenue	80,000		(74,676)
06/30/2000	Revenue	140,000		65,324
06/30/2000	Bills Paid		106,000	(40,676)
07/01/2000	Bills Paid		139,500	(180,176)
07/05/2000	Payroll		290,000	(470,176)
07/07/2000	Revenue	662,000		191,824
07/15/2000	Revenue	30,000		221,824
07/15/2000	Bills Paid		105,000	116,824
07/17/2000	Revenue	662,000		778,824
07/21/2000	Payroll		290,000	488,824
07/28/2000	Revenue	80,000		568,824
07/31/2000	Revenue	140,000		708,824
07/31/2000	Bills Paid		106,000	602,824
Total		**$3,568,000**	**$3,630,245**	**$602,824**

Note: Some organizations find this report extremely useful in their cash flow management.

Universal Nonprofit
Cash Flow Forecast by Revenue Type
Fiscal Year 2000

Service Type	Revenue Type A				Revenue Type B				Revenue Type C			
	FY 2000 Actual	FY 2001 Forecasted	FY 2002 Forecasted	FY 2003 Forecasted	FY 2000 Actual	FY 2001 Forecasted	FY 2002 Forecasted	FY 2003 Forecasted	FY 2000 Actual	FY 2001 Forecasted	FY 2002 Forecasted	FY 2003 Forecasted
Service 1	$45,000	$44,100	$43,218	$42,354	$29,250	$28,665	$28,091	$27,529	$32,760	$32,104	$31,462	$30,833
Service 2	34,000	36,380	38,927	41,651	22,100	23,647	25,302	27,073	9,945	10,641	11,386	12,183
Service 3	65,000	66,138	67,295	68,473	42,250	42,989	43,741	44,507	24,927	25,363	25,807	26,259
Service 4	41,500	42,952	44,455	46,011	26,975	27,918	28,895	29,907	28,863	29,872	30,918	32,000
Total	$185,500	$189,570	$193,895	$198,489	$120,575	$123,219	$126,029	$129,016	$96,495	$97,980	$99,573	$101,275

Note: This report is very useful for more complicated organizations.

EXHIBIT A.3 Sample Comprehensive Cash Accounts Summary

Universal Nonprofit
Comprehensive Cash Accounts Summary
August 2000

| DATE | SOURCE | OPENING CASH BALANCE | CASH INFLOWS | | | | | CASH OUTFLOWS | | | | ENDING CASH BALANCE |
			DEPOSITS	DIRECT DEPOSITS	INTEREST INCOME	CREDIT LINE	TOTAL DEPOSITS	GENERAL ACCOUNT TRANSFERS	PAYROLL ACCOUNT	OTHER TRANSACTIONS	TOTAL WITHDRAWALS	
8/1/00	General Account	$1,110,762	$—	$—	$—	$—	$—	$212,000	$—	$—	$212,000	$898,762
8/1/00	General Account	898,762						87,000			87,000	811,762
8/2/00	Deposit	811,762	313,625				313,625					1,125,387
8/4/00	Deposit	1,125,387	7,471				7,471					1,132,858
8/8/00	Deposit	1,132,858	17,020				17,020					1,149,878
8/8/00	General Account	1,149,878						155,000			155,000	994,878
8/9/00	Deposit	994,878	38,711				38,711					1,033,589
8/11/00	Payroll Account	1,033,589							133,057		133,057	900,532
8/11/00	Payroll Taxes	900,532								96,677	96,677	803,855
8/11/00	Direct Withdrawal	803,855								92,450	92,450	711,405
8/11/00	Transfer	711,405								75,000	75,000	636,405
8/15/00	General Account	636,405						60,000			60,000	576,405
8/15/00	Deposit	576,405	300,645				300,645					877,050
8/17/00	Deposit	877,050	1,534				1,534					878,584
8/20/00	Direct Deposit	878,584		71,296			71,296					949,880
8/22/00	Deposit	949,880	18,776				18,776					968,656
8/22/00	General Account	968,656						209,000			209,000	759,656
8/22/00	General Account	759,656						195,000			195,000	564,656
8/25/00	Payroll Account	564,656							325,000		325,000	239,656
Total			$697,782	$71,296	$—	$—	$769,078	$918,000	$458,057	$264,127	$1,640,184	$239,656

Note: This report is most beneficial to organizations with multiple sources of cash.

EXHIBIT A.4   **Sample Cash Forecast by Funding Source**

Universal Nonprofit
Cash Forecast by Funding Source
Fiscal Year 2000

FUNDING SOURCE	FY 1999 FORECASTED	FY 1999 ACTUAL	FY 2000 FORECASTED	FY 2000 ACTUAL	FY 2001 FORECASTED
Funding Source 1	$150,000	$150,000	$165,000	$157,500	$169,950
Funding Source 2	175,000	145,000	192,500	152,250	198,275
Funding Source 3	125,000	117,500	137,500	123,375	141,625
Total	$450,000	$412,500	$495,000	$433,125	$509,850

EXHIBIT A.5   **Sample Estimate of Percentages of Total Service Mix and Collections by Service Type**

Universal Nonprofit
Estimated Percentages of Total Service Mix
and Collections by Service Type
Fiscal Year 2000

SERVICE TYPE	ESTIMATED PERCENTAGE OF TOTAL SERVICE MIX	ESTIMATED PERCENTAGE OF TOTAL COLLECTIONS
Counseling	40	45
Tutoring	15	13
Transportation	45	42
Total	100	100

Sample Cash Inflow and Outflow Variances Report Format

Universal Nonprofit
Cash Inflow and Outflow Variances Report
Fiscal Year 2000

FISCAL YEAR 2000 ACTUAL

	1999 ACTUAL	2000 APPROVED BUDGET	2000 ADJUSTED BUDGET	FIRST QUARTER	SECOND QUARTER	THIRD QUARTER	FOURTH QUARTER	YEAR-TO-DATE TOTAL	2000 CASH FORECAST	DOLLAR VARIANCE	PERCENTAGE VARIANCE
CASH INFLOWS:											
Fees for Service	___	___	___	___	___	___	___	___	___	___	___
Grants and Contracts	___	___	___	___	___	___	___	___	___	___	___
Other Revenue	___	___	___	___	___	___	___	___	___	___	___
Total Cash Inflows	___	___	___	___	___	___	___	___	___	___	___
CASH OUTFLOWS:											
Salaries and Wages	___	___	___	___	___	___	___	___	___	___	___
Fringe Benefits	___	___	___	___	___	___	___	___	___	___	___
Supplies and General	___	___	___	___	___	___	___	___	___	___	___
Total Cash Outflows	___	___	___	___	___	___	___	___	___	___	___
NET CASH AVAILABLE	___	___	___	___	___	___	___	___	___	___	___

Note: All variances between actual and budgeted cash in excess of 3 percent will require an explanation and a corrective action plan.

EXHIBIT A.7   **Sample Variance Analysis and Explanation Form**

Universal Nonprofit
_____ Budget
Variance Analysis and Explanation

Department: _____
Cost Center: _____
Prepared by: _____
Date: _____

CASH INFLOWS:

Cost Center	Account Description	Quarter Ended: Year-to-Date Variance	Year Ending: Projected Annual Variance
_____	_____	_____	_____
_____	_____	_____	_____
_____	_____	_____	_____
_____	_____	_____	_____
_____	_____	_____	_____
_____	_____	_____	_____
_____	_____	_____	_____
_____	_____	_____	_____

Total Cash Inflows   _____   _____

CASH OUTFLOWS:

Cost Center	Account Description	Quarter Ended: Year-to-Date Variance	Year Ending: Projected Annual Variance
_____	_____	_____	_____
_____	_____	_____	_____
_____	_____	_____	_____
_____	_____	_____	_____
_____	_____	_____	_____
_____	_____	_____	_____
_____	_____	_____	_____
_____	_____	_____	_____

Total Cash Outflows   _____   _____

VARIANCE EXPLANATIONS

Cost Center	Program	Explanation
_____	_____	_____
_____	_____	_____
_____	_____	_____
_____	_____	_____
_____	_____	_____

Note: This form is useful for larger organizations.

EXHIBIT A.8   **Sample Cash Flow Impact Disclosure Form for New Positions**

Universal Nonprofit
Request for New Position—Cash Flow Impact Disclosure
Fiscal Year _____

Department: _____   Date Proposed: _____
Prepared by: _____   Effective Date: _____
Title:

Approved by: _____
Date: _____

Position Title: _____   ☐ Union   ☐ Non-Union
Total Hours: _____   Cost Center: _____

Describe the tasks and responsibilities of the requested position.

_____
_____
_____
_____

Demonstrate the need for the position, including relevance to the organization's mission and strategic plan. Use relevant workload statistics or other documented evidence of the need for the services to be provided.

_____
_____
_____
_____

Cash Flow Impact

CASH INFLOWS:

	Fiscal Year 1	Fiscal Year 2	Fiscal Year 3
1. _____	_____	_____	_____
2. _____	_____	_____	_____
3. _____	_____	_____	_____
4. _____	_____	_____	_____
5. _____	_____	_____	_____
Total Cash Inflows	_____	_____	_____

CASH OUTFLOWS:

	Fiscal Year 1	Fiscal Year 2	Fiscal Year 3
1. Salary and Wages	_____	_____	_____
2. Fringe Benefits	_____	_____	_____
3. Supplies	_____	_____	_____
4. Capital Equipment	_____	_____	_____
5. Other	_____	_____	_____
Total Cash Outflows	_____	_____	_____

EXHIBIT A.9   **Sample New Program or Program Change Request Form**

Universal Nonprofit

_____ Budget

Request for New Program or Change to Existing Program

Department: _____   Date Proposed: _____
Prepared by: _____   Effective Date: _____
Title: _____

Approved by: _____
Date: _____
Program Title: _____

☐ New Program   ☐ Change to Existing Program

Program Summary and Needs Analysis

_____

_____

_____

Anticipated Benefits and Outcomes

_____

_____

_____

Cash Flow Impact

INCREMENTAL CASH INFLOWS:

	Fiscal Year 1	Fiscal Year 2	Fiscal Year 3
1. _____	_____	_____	_____
2. _____	_____	_____	_____
3. _____	_____	_____	_____
4. _____	_____	_____	_____
Total Cash Inflows	_____	_____	_____

INCREMENTAL CASH OUTFLOWS:

	Fiscal Year 1	Fiscal Year 2	Fiscal Year 3
1. Salaries and Wages	_____	_____	_____
2. Fringe Benefits	_____	_____	_____
3. Supplies and General	_____	_____	_____
4. Services	_____	_____	_____
Total Cash Outflows	_____	_____	_____

Is capital equipment requested   ☐ Yes   ☐ No
in the capital budget?

New Positions Required (Complete a cash flow impact disclosure form for each—see Exhibit A.8):

_____

B Sample Grant Checklist for Cash Flow Planning and Management

The checklist that follows will help organizations keep track of all of the steps involved in obtaining and managing grant moneys, planning and managing the activities for which the grants were awarded, and complying with funding-source requirements. Attending to all details of grant management will increase the likelihood of timely receipt of grant moneys. In addition, it will increase the likelihood that funding sources will continue to fund the programs or activities.

Not all of the steps listed will apply to every grant or to every grant-funded activity. Organizations should customize the checklist to reflect the circumstances and requirements of each grant, grantor, and grant-funded activity.

EXHIBIT B.1   **Sample Grant Checklist for Cash Flow Planning and Management**

GRANT MANAGEMENT PLAN STEP	RESPONSIBLE PERSON(S)	DATE DUE
A. Receipt of Official Funding-Approval Notification		
1. Review the award, notice, or contract carefully to ensure understanding of all conditions of the award, especially those applying to requesting cash and reporting expenditures.	_____	_____
2. Write or modify job descriptions for each staff position associated with carrying out the purpose for which the grant was awarded.	_____	_____
3. Prepare and place ads to recruit any additional staff that will be necessary to carry out grant-funded activities (do this after the grant is received).	_____	_____

EXHIBIT B.1 **Sample Grant Checklist for Cash Flow Planning and Management** *(continued)*

GRANT MANAGEMENT PLAN STEP	RESPONSIBLE PERSON(S)	DATE DUE
B. Staff Training and Development		
1. Design, schedule, conduct, and evaluate any staff training needed to carry out the program or purpose for which grant moneys were received.		
2. Include staff of other programs, as needed, to support cross-training and collaboration.		
C. Facilities, Equipment, and Supplies		
1. Review all bidding requirements and procurement policies and procedures.		
2. Identify amount of funds available.		
3. Identify potential vendors.		
4. Purchase needed equipment and supplies.		
5. Seek satisfactory facilities when necessary.		
6. Negotiate with potential landlords.		
7. Agree on terms and sign leases.		
D. Intra-Agency Linkages and Working Relationships		
1. Identify other relevant in-house programs and activities.		
2. Review relationship of grant-funded activities to goals, objectives, and design of related programs with staff of those programs.		
3. Determine mutual interests, functions, and roles.		
4. Develop procedures and forms for collaboration and involvement in grant-funded activities.		
5. Create a written record of agreed-on roles, linkages, and procedures.		
E. Interagency Linkages and Working Relationships		
1. Identify relevant outside agencies, programs, and activities.		
2. Initiate contact with relevant outside parties and review grant-funded activity program goals, objectives, and design with them.		

EXHIBIT B.1	Sample Grant Checklist for Cash Flow Planning and Management *(continued)*

GRANT MANAGEMENT PLAN STEP	RESPONSIBLE PERSON(S)	DATE DUE
3. Determine mutual interests, functions, and roles.	_____	_____
4. Form advisory or coordinating groups.	_____	_____
5. Plan and negotiate linkages and collaboration.	_____	_____
6. Create referral and collaboration procedures and forms.	_____	_____
7. Confirm agreements in writing to create a written record of agreed-on roles, linkages, and procedures.	_____	_____
8. Identify other relevant organizations to join or meetings to attend.	_____	_____
9. Identify an in-house liaison to maintain ongoing communication with managers or executives of collaborating agencies.	_____	_____
10. Identify an in-house liaison to maintain ongoing communication with program or service representatives of collaborating agencies.	_____	_____
F. Development of Evaluation Designs and Materials		
1. Identify funding-source evaluation requirements.	_____	_____
2. Identify in-house evaluation requirements.	_____	_____
3. Assign responsibilities for gathering and analysis of evaluation data.	_____	_____
4. Identify evaluation standards for each goal and objective.	_____	_____
5. Identify evaluation methods for each goal and objective.	_____	_____
6. Identify evaluation data sources for each goal and objective.	_____	_____
7. Develop needed evaluation materials.	_____	_____
8. Create evaluation procedures and forms as needed.	_____	_____
9. Integrate data collection and evaluation requirements with any existing database capabilities.	_____	_____

EXHIBIT B.1 **Sample Grant Checklist for Cash Flow Planning and Management** *(continued)*

GRANT MANAGEMENT PLAN STEP	RESPONSIBLE PERSON(S)	DATE DUE
10. Familiarize staff with grant-related evaluation requirements, procedures, forms, and responsibilities.	_____	_____
G. Record Keeping and Reporting		
1. Identify funding-source reporting requirements.	_____	_____
2. Identify in-house reporting requirements.	_____	_____
3. Assign data-gathering and reporting responsibilities.	_____	_____
4. Create or revise record-keeping forms, procedures, and responsibilities as needed.	_____	_____
5. Integrate data collection and reporting requirements with any existing database capabilities.	_____	_____
6. Familiarize staff with record-keeping and reporting forms, procedures, and responsibilities.	_____	_____
7. Begin data collection and analysis.	_____	_____
8. Prepare and submit required monthly in-house reports.	_____	_____
9. Prepare and submit funding-source reports and other reports as required.	_____	_____
H. Outreach		
1. Identify target groups for participation in grant-funded activity.	_____	_____
2. Develop outreach plans and materials.	_____	_____
3. Orient and train outreach personnel as needed.	_____	_____
4. Conduct outreach activities, and monitor results regularly.	_____	_____
5. Review and revise outreach plan and activities as needed.	_____	_____
I. Public Information and Public Relations		
1. Prepare and disseminate a press release on the grant award.	_____	_____
2. Identify and plan for other public information or public relations opportunities.	_____	_____

EXHIBIT B.1	Sample Grant Checklist for Cash Flow Planning and Management *(continued)*

GRANT MANAGEMENT PLAN STEP	RESPONSIBLE PERSON(S)	DATE DUE
3. Issue press releases and press kits, gain coverage for events and photo opportunities, and disseminate relevant publications and reports.	_____	_____
J. Grant Use Monitoring and Control		
1. Measure progress against this grant management plan (a program director with responsibility for grant-funded activity should meet regularly with an in-house supervisor to do this).	_____	_____
2. Identify, plan, and take corrective action as needed.	_____	_____
3. Request any needed program or activity modifications in writing, including extension, if allowed and needed.	_____	_____
K. Budget Monitoring and Control		
1. Prepare internal operating budget for the program or activity using grant funds.	_____	_____
2. Disseminate operating budget as appropriate.	_____	_____
3. Maintain ongoing communication between the director of the program or activity using grant funds and the finance department regarding expenses, budget, and finances.	_____	_____
4. Identify, plan, and take corrective action as required.	_____	_____
5. Request budget modifications in writing as needed.	_____	_____
6. Request carryover of funds if allowed and needed.	_____	_____
L. Other Major Activities, Objectives, or Milestones		
1. Identify specific action steps for reaching each goal.	_____	_____
2. Create or modify relevant policies and procedures as needed for grant-related services and activities.	_____	_____
3. Identify and schedule access to needed outside services (such as printing or consultants).	_____	_____

EXHIBIT B.1   Sample Grant Checklist for Cash Flow Planning and Management (continued)

GRANT MANAGEMENT PLAN STEP	RESPONSIBLE PERSON(S)	DATE DUE
4. Create needed materials.		
M. Grant Activity and Financial Evaluation		
1. Begin collection and analysis of evaluation data.		
2. Prepare and submit required in-house evaluations.		
3. Prepare and submit interim and final funding-source evaluations as required.		
N. Continued Grant Management		
1. Identify in-house liaisons to maintain ongoing communication with funding-source managers, executives, and other representatives.		
2. Prepare and submit all in-house and funding-source reports on time.		
3. Gather and analyze evaluation data regularly.		
4. Prepare and submit all evaluation reports as required.		
5. Identify potential funding sources for program refunding and continuation or expansion.		
6. Prepare and submit proposals for program refunding and continuation or expansion.		
7. Negotiate with potential refunding sources as needed.		
O. Cash Flow Management		
1. Prepare a cash flow forecast.		
2. Identify timing of cash receipts (monthly, quarterly, or other).		
3. Identify timing of cash disbursements (monthly, quarterly, or other) for all items in the budget.		
4. Determine any fiscal periods when cash flow may be deficient.		
5. Devise a strategy to correct any projected cash flow deficiencies.		